KANSAS CITY

Royals

Facts & Trivia™

by
Mark Stallard

D1530517

GC CASS COUNTY PUBLIC LIBRARY
400 E. MECHANIC
HARRISONVILLE, MO 64701

KAW VALLEY
BOOKS

Overland Park, KS 66225

ISBN-13: 978-1492250708
ISBN-10: 1492250708

Library of Congress Control Number: 2013915921

Kaw Valley Books
P.O. Box 26242
Overland Park, KS 66225

Contents

KANSAS CITY

Royals

Facts & Trivia™

To my little sluggers,

Walt & Nate

Introduction

Of all the great moments in the Royals history, one of my favorites is one I missed.

In the spring of 1977 I was finishing my freshman year in college and trying very hard to compile acceptable grades. My first go around with finals the semester before had been sub-par, and I was determined to improve. So when one of my friends offered me a free pass to a Royals game two days before my hardest test, I didn't think twice about turning it down; I *had* to get an A on the upcoming test. Baseball could wait.

One of my best friends, Mike O'Connell, took my pass instead. Mike was never much of a baseball fan, but he has always been great at seizing spontaneous moments. He gladly went to the game, maybe more to heckle the players and drink a few beers than enjoy baseball. I stayed home and pretended to study.

I don't remember what I was doing when Mike returned from the game; maybe I was studying—though I doubt it—and more than likely I was watching TV or sleeping when he burst into the room.

"A no-hitter!" Mike screamed. "We saw a no-hitter!"

Yeah, right. He always tried to pull stuff like that on me, so I knew he was joking.

"A no-hitter! *You* missed it, and *I* saw it! " I'll never forget the look of satisfaction on his face.

Okay, enough. Who won the game? What was the score?

"I'm serious. Man, the crowd went wild and the team went crazy. It was the greatest game I've ever seen!"

Okay, smart guy. So who threw this no-hitter? Splittorff? Leonard?

"No, it was . . . ," *and he couldn't remember the name of the Royals pitcher!* "But it was a no-hitter!"

Jim Colborn had treated Mike to the no-hit gem against the Texas Rangers, the first Royals pitcher to do so in Royals Stadium. For the last 20 years Mike has occasionally mentioned the game and rubbed it in a little ("You know, I didn't really watch that much of the game"), and sometimes he'll tell me how I'm responsible for helping him find joy in baseball, just because he got to see that no-hit game. "I've never heard a ball pop in the catcher's mitt the way it did that night," he told me recently.

The Royals have had a lot of great moments in their relatively short history, and I've seen almost all of them. From Opening Day games to the World Series, I've been at the ballpark numerous times to watch and glory in the team's achievements. When that wasn't possible, I've watched them on TV. But I've always regretted the one game I missed, Colborn's no-hitter. Sometimes we make the right choice, only to find out later it was wrong. As for that test, I got a C. Oh, well.

I hope you enjoy the facts, dates, quotes, numbers and names within these pages. Have fun with them. The Royals have been a fun team, a great team, and unfortunately, at times a bad team. But that's also part of baseball.

Play ball!

ROYALS
FACTS

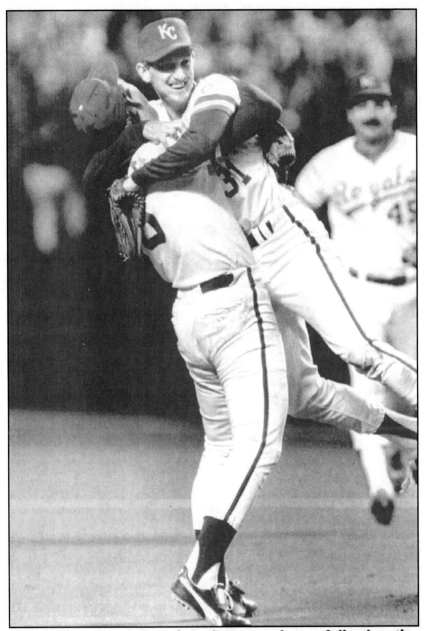

George Brett and Bret Saberhagen embrace following the Royals Game 7 win over the Cardinals that clinched the 1985 World Series.

A Real Baseball Team
A Brief Overview of Kansas City Baseball

How could so much good be the by-product of so much bad? Years of losing, last-place teams and, not just bad ownership, but threatening ownership, left the baseball fans of Kansas City with more than a bad taste in their mouths. The A's weren't just bad, they were usually atrocious; and they weren't bad in a loveable way like the Mets were in their early years. They were bad so that you hated them, their ugly green uniforms, their obnoxious owner and that stupid mule. If ever a team deserved a city's contemptuous wrath and indifference, it was the Kansas City A's.

When Charlie Finley, the A's pompous owner, announced his intentions to move the team to Oakland at the conclusion of the 1967 season, it was a bittersweet thing for the city's fans. The hated man was taking his hated team away, but he was also taking Major League Baseball away.

Dick Howser, Bret Saberhagen and George Brett (all in Royals' uniforms) talk about the 1985 World Series win with TV Analyst Reggie Jackson and team owners Avron Fogelman and Ewing Kauffman.

3

Enter Missouri Senator Stuart Symington and Kansas City Mayor Ilus Davis. If Kansas City wasn't given another Major League franchise immediately, Senator Symington threatened, then maybe another investigation by Congress into baseball's antitrust exemption would be warranted. Mayor Davis simply threatened court injunctions to keep the A's in Kansas City. This double-edged political assault worked, and the American League promised Kansas City a new franchise for the 1969 season.

So Finley, who Symington described as "one of the most disreputable characters ever to enter the American sports scene," packed up his green uniforms and headed for the West Coast. And on January 11, 1968 the American League awarded Ewing Kauffman the new franchise for $5.5 million. Kansas City had Major League Baseball again, or maybe for the first time. It was a team worth waiting for.

Unions, Cowboys and Blues

Kansas City's experience with Major League Baseball before the Royals was not good, and that includes more than just the A's. In 1884, Kansas City got its first Major League team when the Unions were formed and admitted into the Union Association to replace the defunct Altoona club. A success financially, the Unions were horrible on the field, fashioning a miserable 16-63 record. But the club didn't disband until the league folded the following winter.

The city's second entry in the Majors was the Cowboys, a last-minute addition to the National League in 1886. This team was also bad, and might have actually been worse than their 30-91 record. The long distances other teams had to travel and poor attendance by KC's unruly fans doomed the Cowboys. When Pittsburgh was accepted into the NL the following season, Kansas City was expelled. Attempts by the Cowboys owners to move into the American Association failed, and the team died.

The Blues were the third Kansas City entry into the Majors, entering the American Association in 1888 (the league was considered a major then). But like their two woeful predecessors, the Blues were a poor team and received shaky support. After the 1889 season, the Blues fell victim to the politics of baseball. After resigning from the AA the team joined the Western Association, a minor league.

The upstart Federal League presented the last real challenge to baseball's Major Leagues in 1914, and included the Kansas City Packers. This team was mediocre and never really shook being compared to the minor league Blues. The league itself suffered from several financial woes, and after losing huge amounts of money, the Feds folded following the 1915 season. Kansas City didn't have Major League Baseball for another 40 years.

The World Famous Kansas City Monarchs

Kansas City was without a Major League team from 1916 thru 1954, but they might have had something better: the Kansas City Monarchs, one of the greatest Negro League teams. Starting in 1920, the Monarchs played in two different leagues, operated as an independent, and had some of the greatest players ever wearing their uniforms. Pitching great Satchel Paige helped put the Monarchs on the baseball map, and while the Kansas City Blues of the American Association (minor league) were always excellent, the Monarchs gave the city a touch of baseball class only a Major League franchise could give. The demise of the Negro League teams came when baseball finally integrated in 1947.

The 1934 Kansas City Monarchs

The Kansas City A's

The less said about the A's, the better. During their 13-year stint in Kansas City, the A's were the worst team in the history of baseball for the length of existence of the team, never finishing higher than sixth place (which it did only once). They finished last in the American League five times and never won more than 73 games in a season. The best that can be said about the A's is that the team brought Major League baseball back to Kansas City, and then left.

Lasting Legacy of Winning

The Royals are the most successful expansion team ever, with 2,407 wins (through 1998) in the franchise's history and an all-time winning percentage of .510. They are the only expansion team with a winning percentage above .500! They have won six division championships, two American League pennants and a World Series championship. The Royals made success a part of the franchise's tradition, and for the better part of the team's existence, have always been a front runner in the league.

During the team's inaugural season in 1969, it was apparent this Kansas City baseball club was going to be run differently from former KC teams. The Royals won their first game ever, and by 1971 posted an impressive 85 wins and second place finish in the AL West. Smart trades (Hal McRae, John Mayberry and Amos Otis) and good draft choices (George Brett, Willie Wilson, Dennis Leonard) led to more success. The team moved into Royals Stadium in 1973, and by 1975 Manager Whitey Herzog had the club ready to challenge for a division title. The team joined

KC Shortstop Jackie Hernandez looks on in the Royals first-ever game as Jerry Adair puts a tag on the Twins' Rod Carew.

George Brett

baseball's elite the following season and won the first three straight division titles. The American League Championship proved elusive, though, as the Royals lost to the Yankees three years in a row.

The team slipped a bit in 1979, but under new manager Jim Frey—with the help of George Brett's MVP season—the Royals returned to the ALCS in 1980. This time the team prevailed against the Yankees and

The 1972 Kansas City Royals

brought the Kansas City its first World Series. Although the team lost to the Phillies in the Series, it was one of the city's greatest baseball season.

Problems followed success. After winning half of the division title in 1981, the team slipped to second in 1982 and 1983. But the club was able to revamp the pitching staff with Bret Saberhagen, Danny Jackson, Mark Gubicza and Charlie Leibrandt. The Royals rebounded to win the AL West in 1984, and then produced the city's greatest baseball season ever with a World Championship in 1985.

The Royals have floundered a bit since that World Series win. Manager Dick Howser left the team in the middle of the 1986 season when he was diagnosed with a brain tumor, and passed away the following summer. The team still challenged for the division title almost every year through 1994, but was never able to capture another crown.

Ewing Kauffman, the club's only majority owner since it's beginning, passed away in 1993 and left the team in the hands of its Board of Directors. Rising salaries and poor player moves have kept the club from contending since 1994.

The end of the 1990s promises better things for Kansas City baseball. An owner for the Royals will soon be in place and hopefully a new, positive direction for the franchise will be established. Johnny Damon, Kevin Appier, Jeff King and Jeff Montgomery have been quality players for the

Royals, and with each new season, hope always springs eternal.

The Royals have accomplished much in their short history: the World Series win, George Brett's batting titles, Bret Saberhagen and David Cone's Cy Young Awards, Frank White's Gold Gloves, and the numerous division titles. They have also provided Kansas City with something it had long deserved: a true Major League franchise.

The winning tradition established by the Kansas City Royals is something that will last forever. With a little luck and hard work, that tradition will again flourish.

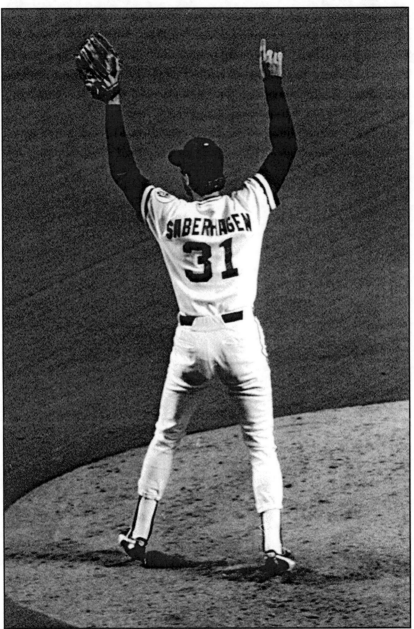

Bret Saberhagen, Kansas City's two-time Cy Young Award winner, watches the final out of the 1985 World Series.

Royals Chronology

1968

January 11 - Ewing Kauffman becomes the owner of Kansas City's new American League franchise.

March 21 - The Board of Directors selects "Royals" as the team nickname after a study of more than 17,000 suggestions from the Kansas City area fans.

April 25 - Free agent Gerald Lyscio becomes the first player to sign with the Royals.

June 6 - Kansas City selects 25 players in baseball's Free Agent Draft, the first such draft for the Royals. The team did not have a first round selection.

July 11 - Ground is broken for Kansas City's Harry S. Truman Sports Complex.

September 5 - The first season ticket drive is launched. First-day sales total an encouraging 2,156 season tickets.

September 9 - Joe Gordon is hired to manage Royals.

October 15 - Roger Nelson is the first player chosen by the Royals in the American League expansion draft. Other top picks include Joe Foy, Jim Rooker and Joe Keough. Future Hall-of-Famer Hoyt Wilhelm is chosen in the 25th round.

December 12 - Hoyt Wilhelm is traded to California for Ed Kirkpatrick and Dennis Paeke.

Royals owner Ewing Kauffman speaks before the club's first game at Municipal Stadium in 1969.

1969

February 21 - Forty-six players participate in first workout ever. Fort Myers, Florida, is the site.

March 6 - Kansas City collects 16 hits but loses exhibition opener to Montreal, 9-8.

March 8 - Kansas City uses home runs by Pat Kelly and Chuck Harrison to win its first game, 2-1, over Washington, at Fort Myers. Roger Nelson, Dave Morehead and Jerry Cram combine to pitch a six-hitter.

> *They're spirited, clean-cut young-sters (one of the youngest Major League squads ever). Their attitude as a team is incomparably high. They help on another and cheer each other's successes.*
>
> **Ewing Kauffman, 1969**

April 1 - Lou Piniella comes to the Royals from Seattle in exchange for Steve Whitaker and John Gelnar.

April 5 - The Royals play their first game in Kansas City, an exhibition with St. Louis, but lose, 1-0.

> *One of the expansion teams will have the privilege of being the most successful franchise in 1969. Kansas City will probably be it.*
>
> **Sports Illustrated's Baseball Preview, 1969**

April 7 - Season-ticket sales close at 6,805, a then all-time American League record.

The 1969 Kansas City Royals

April 8 - Joe Keough's bases-loaded pinch single with one out in the 12th inning scores Joe Foy, giving the Royals a win in their American League opener against Minnesota, 4-3. Attendance at Municipal Stadium is 17,688. Moe Drabowsky notches the win for KC.

April 9 -The Royals and Twins play for 17 innings before KC prevails, 4-3. Tom Burgmeier gets the win.

April 13 - Mike Fiore hits the first home run for the Royals, a solo shot over the right-field wall at the Oakland Coliseum.

May 4 - Bob Oliver goes 6-for-6 as the Royals pound the Angels, 15-1.

July 16 - Ellie Rodriguez becomes the first Royal selected for the American League All-Star team.

August 2 - Ewing Kauffman gives a commitment letter to Jackson County

Bob Oliver

Court to lease the baseball stadium in the new sports complex. The lease is for 25 years, with an option for 10 years.

August 26 - Omaha wins the American Association championship, giving KC its first farm club title. No other first-year club in modern history has had a minor league champion above Class B.

September 5 - Bill Butler K's 10 batters for the third time this season, but the Royals lose to Seattle, 5-4.

September 11 - Ewing Kauffman announces plans for a Baseball Academy in Florida. Syd Thrift is named director.

October 2 - The Royals end their first season with a 69-93 record, one win shy of the modern-day record for victories by a first-year team. They finish fourth in the American League West.

Bill Butler

Lou Piniella, the 1969 American League Rookie of the Year.

October 8 - Joe Gordon resigns as the Royals manager. Charlie Metro is named to manage the club in 1970.

October 24 - Paul Splittorff is promoted to the major league roster, becoming the first player signed originally by the Royals to reach the major league level.

November 26 - Sweet Lou. Lou Piniella is elected by the Baseball Writers Association of America (BBWAA) as the 1969 American League Rookie of the Year.

December 3 - In one of the club's greatest trades, Kansas City sends Joe Foy to the Mets for Amos Otis and Bob Johnson.

1970

January 20 - Ground is broken for the Minor League Complex and Baseball Academy in Sarasota, FL.

April 7 - Opening Day in Kansas City. Amos Otis plays in his first game for the Royals, but the A's win at Municipal Stadium, beating Wally Bunker, 6-4.

June 9 - Manager Charlie Metro is fired and Bob Lemon is named as the club's new skipper. The Royals win, 8-2, over the Senators.

June 13 - The Royals acquire Cookie Rojas from the Cardinals for Fred Rico.

July 1 - In another key move, Kansas City picks up Ted Abernathy from the Cardinals for Chris Zachary.

July 11 - Lou Piniella starts an 18-game hitting streak against Chicago. Bill Butler hurls a shutout as the Royals win, 4-0.

July 14 - Amos Otis becomes first Royal to play in an All-Star Game. He plays the last six innings at Cincinnati as the NL beats the AL, 5-4, in 12 innings.

Amos Otis

Cookie Rojas and Fred Patek

August 23 - Bob Johnson strikes out 12 Red Sox en route to winning, 4-3.

September 21 - Jim York becomes first player originally signed by the Royals to appear in a major league game. His 4-2/3 innings of 1-run relief earns him an 8-2 win at Chicago.

September 23 - Paul Splittorff makes his debut for the Royals with a 6-0 loss to the White Sox in Chicago.

October 1 - Minnesota's Jim Kaat shuts out the Royals, 4-0, in the last game of the season. KC finishes with a 65-97 mark and another fourth place finish in the AL West.

December 2 - Another piece of the future falls into place when the Royals get Fred Patek, Jerry May and Bruce Dal Canton from the Pirates for Bob Johnson, Jack Hernandez and Jimmy Campanis.

1971

January 21 - The Royals' Baseball Academy is officially dedicated.

April 6 - Kansas City's Dick Drago beats the Angels, 4-1, in the season opener at California.

May 31 -The Royals move into second place in the Western Division by sweeping a doubleheader in Boston, 7-3 and 9-4, and hold it the remainder of the year.

June 7 -The Royals select an 18-year-old shortstop from El Segundo, California, named George Brett as their second pick in the Free Agent Draft.

> *I want to do everything, so that when The Man (Ewing kauffman) looks at me he'll want to pay me $100,000.*
> **Amos Otis, 1971**

June 14 - The Royals win for the 12th time in 13 games as Mike Hedlund beats the Yankees, 4-1.

July 9 - Freddie Patek becomes the first Royal to hit for the cycle. The Royals defeat Minnesota, 6-3.

August 11 - Paul Splittorff throws a one-hitter on route to beating the Senators, 1-0, in Washington.

September 7 - Amos Otis collects four hits and steals five bases at Municipal Stadium as the Royals defeat Milwaukee, 4-3.

September 26 - The Royals win their 85th game of the season, a 5-3 decision over Minnesota in the second game of a doubleheader on the final day of the season. They finish second in the AL West.

Paul Splittorff

December 2 - Big John comes to KC. The Royals acquire John Mayberry and Dave Grangaard from the Houston Astros for Lance Clemons and Jim York.

1972

April 15 - A short players strike—the first of its kind—delays the start of the season. The Royals open with a win, beating Chicago at Municipal Stadium, 2-1, in 11 innings.

May 5 -The Royals trade Bob Oliver to the Angels for Tom Murphy.

April 23 - Roger Nelson comes within five outs of tossing a no-hitter against Boston. Ben Ogilvie's one-out single in the eighth is the only safety off Nelson as the Royals win at Municipal, 3-0.

April 30 - In a 16-inning affair, Cleveland defeats the Royals, 5-3, in the first game of a doubleheader. Al Fitzmorris takes the loss.

May 17 - The Royals battle Texas for 18 innings at Municipal Stadium before falling, 4-3. Ted Abernathy takes the loss for Kansas City. The game is tied for the longest in Royals history.

Roger Nelson

August 23 - Roger Nelson one-hits the Red Sox at Municipal Stadium. The Royals win, 3-0.

August 27 - The Royals drop another 16-inning game, this time to the Yankees, 9-8. Bruce Dal Canton takes the loss.

October 3 - Bob Lemon gets the ax and Jack McKeon is named manager for 1973.

October 4 - The Royals win the last game played in Municipal Stadium. Roger Nelson beats Texas, 4-0, with a two-hitter. Attendance is a mere 7,329. The Royals finish the year with a 76-78 record and a fourth-place finish in the AL West.

Jack McKeon

October 25 - KC sends Jim Rooker to the Pirates for Gene Garber.

December 2 - Another great trade. KC gets Hal McRae and Wayne Simpson from the Reds for Roger Nelson and Richie Scheinblum.

1973

March 23 - Steve Busby hurls six innings and Doug Bird three to give the Royals their first no-hit game, a 4-1 spring training victory over Detroit at Fort Myers, Florida.

April 6 - Nolan Ryan beats Steve Busby as the Royals drop the season opener to the Angels in Anaheim, 3-2.

April 10 - Despite 39-degree weather, a crowd of 39,464 fans attends the inaugural game at Royals Stadium. Kansas City easily beats Texas, 12-1. John Mayberry homers, and Paul Splittorff is the winning pitcher.

April 27 - Steve Busby hurls the first no-hitter in Royals history, a 3-0 triumph in Detroit's Tiger Stadium. Busby struck out four and walked six.

June 12 - Frank White makes his debut in a Royals uniform against the Orioles in Baltimore. Kansas City loses, 6-4.

Steve Busby

July 24 - Kansas City hosts the 40th anniversary All-Star Game. A then Kansas City record crowd of 40,849 sees the National League prevail, 7-1. Amos Otis and John Mayberry shine in front of the hometown crowd, collecting 3 of the 5 American League hits between them.

August 2 - George Brett is called up from Class AAA Omaha and at 20 years, two months and 18 days is the youngest Royals player to appear in a regular-season game. He singles in his second at-bat.

Frank White

September 3 - Joe Burke is appointed Vice President-Business and becomes a member of the Board of Directors.

September 26 - Paul Splittorff becomes Kansas City's first 20-game winner with a 6-2 triumph over the White Sox in Chicago.

September 30 - Kansas City is shut out in the last game of the season, 3-0. Steve Mingori takes the loss. The Royals finish their fifth season with a record of 88-74 and a second place finish in the AL West.

October 24 - Dick Drago is sent to Boston in exchange for Marty Pattin.

> *The turf should give us a lift because we play half of our games here...I think my range is as good as ever.*
>
> **Cookie Rojas**
> on the artificial turf
> at Royals Stadium

December 7 - The Royals trade Lou Piniella and pitcher Ken Wright to the Yankees for pitcher Lindy McDaniel.

1974

Feb. 23 - The Royals obtain Vada Pinson from the Indians for Barry Raziano and cash.

April 5 - Kansas City drops the season opener to the Twins at home, 6-4. Lindy McDaniel is the losing pitcher for KC.

April 6 - The Royals set a club record for runs scored in their 23-6 win over the Twins.

June 11 - Joe Burke is appointed Executive Vice President and General Manager.

June 19 - Steve Busby hurls the second no-hitter of his career in near-perfect fashion with a 2-0 win over the Brewers in Milwaukee's County Stadium.

> *To me, the no-hitters are in the past. The one against Milwaukee went out when I got beat in my next game.*
>
> **Steve Busby, 1974**

Busby strikes out three and allows only one base runner, a walk to George Scott leading off the second inning.

August 6 - The Royals sign future Hall-of-Famer and free agent Orlando Cepeda to DH for the remainder of the 1974 season.

August 27 - Hal McRae collects six extra-base hits in a double-header against Cleveland to tie a Major League record. The Royals split the twin bill.

> *But in Frank White, I had a kid whom I thought would become one of the greatest second basemen in the history of the game—and I was right.*
>
> **Whitey Herzog**
> ***White Rat*, 1987**

September 14 - Paul Splittorff drops the first game of a double-header to Minnesota, 7-5. It is the Royals seventh loss in a row, and 18th in their last 20 games.

September 26 - Steve Busby records his 22nd win, a 10-1 victory over California.

October 2 - The Royals lose, 5-4, to the White Sox ending the season with a record of 77-85 and a fifth-place finish in the AL West.

1975

January 24 - The Royals sign future Hall-of-Famer Harmon Killebrew after his release from the Minnesota Twins.

April 7 - Nolan Ryan beats Kansas City in Anaheim, 3-2, on Opening Day. Steve Mingori takes the loss.

June 30 - Veteran pitcher Ray Sadecki is picked up by the Royals from the Braves in exchange for Bruce Dal Canton, Norm Angelini and Al Autry.

Harmon Killebrew

July 1 - John Mayberry hits three home runs off Ferguson Jenkins at Arlington Stadium. The Royals still lose to the Rangers, 5-4.

July 24 - Jack McKeon is fired. Whitey Herzog is named manager of the club.

July 25 - Herzog's managerial debut for KC is a good one. The Royals beat Texas at Royals Stadium, 6-3, with Briles getting the win.

September 7 - Royals DH Tony Solaita clubs three home runs against the Angels in California. KC wins, 8-7.

September 10 - The Royals and A's set an American League record by using 42

Tony Solaita

Whitey Herzog

players in a nine-inning game. The A's win, 16-4.

September 26 - The Royals win their 91st game with an 8-6 victory over Texas, the highest victory total to date in Kansas City's Major League history. Leonard gets the win.

> *There was talent—good young talent—all over the place. I knew the team was going to win, and win a lot.*
> **Whitey Herzog, 1975**

September 27 - George Brett collects the last of his league-leading 195 hits. The Royals lose to Texas, 5-4.

September 28 - Kansas City ends the season with a loss to Texas, 3-1. They finish the year with a record of 91-71, second place in AL West.

November 12 - Nelson for Nelson. Infielder Dave Nelson comes to Kansas City from Texas in exchange for pitcher Nelson Briles.

November 10 - Goodbye Killer. The Royals release designated hitter and future Hall-of-Famer Harmon Killebrew.

John Mayberry

1976

April 9 - Kansas City loses on Opening Day to the White Sox in Chicago, 4-0. Paul Splittorff is the losing pitcher for KC.

May 13 - George Brett sets a Major League record by collecting at least three hits for the sixth consecutive game. The Royals beat the White Sox, 13-2.

May 16 - In a trade that will reap big benefits for years to come, Kansas City sends catcher Fran Healy to the Yankees for Larry Gura.

> *George Brett may be the best all-around ballplayer in our league. And unless a bone is sticking out of him, he's ready to play every day.*
>
> **Whitey Herzog, 1976**

May 18 - The Royals climb into the Western Division lead to stay with a 3-1 win over the Texas at Royals Stadium.

August 9 - Largest regular season crowd (to date) in Kansas City baseball history—40,435—watch as the Royals record an 8-2 victory over the Yankees.

August 17 - George Brett steals home in the tenth inning to give the Royals a 4-3 win over the Indians.

September 4 - Willie Wilson plays in his first game for KC. Dennis Leonard shuts out Texas, 7-0.

The 1976 Kansas City Royals
AL West Champs

George Brett

> *I had by this time developed a considerable attachment to the spirited visiting nine, in their powder blue doubleknits, who had now twice come back to tie up this interesting series. Their veteran shortstop, Patek...was having a splendid time of it afield and at the plate...and the whole lineup, although clearly short of power...seemed to be crowded with youngsters who attacked the ball with great confidence and relish. Foremost among these, of course, was George Brett, had begun to look like the hardest out I had seen since my first glimpse of Al Kaline...*
>
> **Roger Angell**
> *Five Seasons*, **1978**
> on the Royals in the 1976 ALCS

September 29 - Herzog turns to Larry Gura to break a four-game losing streak; Gura responds with a brilliant performance that clinches a tie for the Western Division title, winning a 4-0 triumph over the A's at Oakland.

October 1 - The Royals win the West! Despite losing to Minnesota at home, Kansas City clinches its first division championship when the A's lose to California, 2-0.

October 3 - George Brett edges teammate Hal McRae by .001 in a dramatic battle to capture the AL Batting title with a .333 mark. Brett earned his first batting championship by going 3-for-4 and concluding the season with 215 hits, a league high and an all-time Kansas City record. The Royals lose the season finale, 5-3, and finish with a record of 90-72.

Hal McRae

October 9 - ALCS (American League Championship Series) Game 1. The Yankees' Catfish Hunter tosses a five-hitter at the Royals, winning, 4-1, at Royals Stadium. Two Brett errors in the first inning hurt; Gura is the losing pitcher.

October 10 - ALCS Game 2. KC evens the series at one game apiece with a 7-3 victory over New York at Royals Stadium. A Kansas City record (to date) crowd of 41,091 witnesses the win. Splittorff gets the win.

> *...George Brett, on the count of 0-1, socked a middling-deep, medium-high fly ball that landed just within the second or third row of the short right-field seats, for a tying three-run homer...Brett had confirmed himself a great hitter, for if ever a home run was intentional it was this one.*
>
> **Roger Angell**
> ***Five Seasons*, 1978**
> on Brett's game-tying homer in Game 5 of the 1976 ALCS

October 12 - ALCS Game 3. New York wins at Yankee Stadium, 5-3. Hassler loses for KC.

October 13 - ALCS Game 4. The Royals even the series at two games apiece with a 7-4 victory over Catfish Hunter. Bird relieves Gura and gets the win.

October 14 - ALCS Game 5. New York's Chris Chambliss homers in the bottom of the ninth off Mark Littell to send the Royals home for the winter. New York wins the game, 7-6, and the series, 3 games to 2. Late heroics by Brett, who

Larry Gura

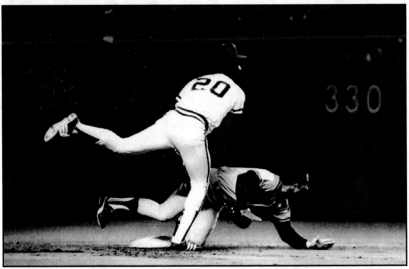

Frank White turns a double play in Game 2 of the 1976 ALCS.

tied the game in the eighth with a three-run home run, went for naught, and New York went to the World Series.

December 6 - Kansas City sends Jamie Quirk, Jim Wohlford and Bob McClure to Milwaukee for Darrell Porter and Jim Colborn.

1977

April 7 - Kansas City opens the season in Detroit, stopping the Tigers, 7-4. Splittorff records the win.

May 14 - Jim Colborn pitches the first no-hitter by a Kansas City pitcher at Royals Stadium, blanking the Texas Rangers, 6-0. Colborn walks just one batter and hits another while facing only 28 batters.

June 1 - John Mayberry hits three home runs off three different pitchers in Toronto. The Royals win, 11-3.

July 2 - Andy Hassler tosses a one-hitter at Cleveland as the Royals win, 1-0.

August 31 - Jim Colborn beats the Rangers at Royals Stadium, 5-4. The win is the first of 16 straight for the team.

Jim Colborn

The 1977 Kansas City Royals
AL West Champs - 102 wins, 60 losses

Al Cowens had a career year in 1977 with a .312 batting average, 23 HRs and 112 RBI.

September 6 - Al Cowens bangs out five hits for the second time during the 1977 season. The Royals win easily over the Mariners, 10-0. Splittorff gets the shutout win for KC.

September 16 - The Mariners beat the Royals, 4-1, ending Kansas City's 16-game winning streak, which began on August 31.

September 23 - Two straight! The Royals clinch their second straight AL West title with a 7-3 win against California. Dennis Leonard notches the victory for the Royals.

October 2 - Dennis Leonard blanks California, 2-0, for KC's 102nd win of the season, a club record and tops in the Majors for 1977.

October 5 - ALCS Game 1. In a rematch of the '76 playoffs, Kansas City takes the upper hand with a 7-2 win against the Yankees in New York. McRae, Mayberry and Cowens homer for the Royals. Splittorff gets the win.

> *I can't believe we lost. There is no way that team over there (Yankees) should beat us.*
> **Freddie Patek**
> after losing Game 5
> of the 1977 ALCS

October 6 - ALCS Game 2. Guidry stops KC as the Royals lose, 6-2. The series is tied one game each.

October 7 - ALCS Game 3. A 6-2 Royals win puts KC up 2 games to 1. Leonard holds the Yanks to four hits in a complete-game victory at Royals Stadium.

October 8 - ALCS Game 4. New York evens things up in the series with a 6-4 win. Gura takes the loss.

> *Just can't believe it. After we got them out in the eighth, I thought we'd be in.*
>
> **Frank White**
> after losing Game 5
> of the 1977 ALCS

> *The big difference between us and the Yankees in the two play-offs was...Sparky Lyle, and I had nobody nearly that effective.*
>
> **Whitey Herzog**
> on the 1976 and 1977 ALCS

October 9 - ALCS Game 5. Ouch! For the second year in a row the

George Brett slides in safely at third with a triple in Game 5 of the 1977 ALCS and receives a kick from Yankees third baseman Graig Nettles. Brett retaliated with a swing at Nettles as Royals third base coach Joe Hiller and umpire Marty Springstead look on. The fight started a bench-clearing brawl between the two teams.

Freddie Patek, Whitey Herzog and Darrell Porter discuss strategy with Paul Splittorff during Game 5 of the 1977 ALCS.

Yankees win the AL pennant in the ninth inning of the final game, this time scoring three runs and winning, 5-3. Dennis Leonard, making a rare relief appearance, takes the loss.

December 9 - The Royals trade for Al Hrabosky, sending Mark Littell and Buck Martinez to St. Louis for the colorful closer.

1978

March 20 - Kansas City rookie Clint Hurdle is pictured on the cover of *Sports Illustrated.* The magazine ballyhoos the young player as a "can't miss" prospect.

April 8 - The Royals drop the season opener at Cleveland, 8-5. Dennis Leonard takes the loss.

May 8 - Birth of the "Herzog Shift." Royals Manager Whitey Herzog positions four players in the outfield at Fenway Park, leaving the second base area empty in an

Al Hrabosky

attempt to stifle Red Sox power hitter Jim Rice's productivity. The shift fails and Red Sox prevail, 8-4.

June 1 - Jim Colborn is traded to the Mariners for Steve Braun.

June 4 - Darrell Porter raps out five hits against the White Sox at Royals Stadium. Kansas City thrashes Chicago, 13-2.

July 21 - Paul Splittorff shuts out Boston, 9-0, for his 100th career win.

July 25 - The Royals lose to the Yankees at Royals Stadium, ending their 10-game win streak.

September 26 - Gura beats the Mariners, 4-1, and the Royals clinch the AL West for the third straight year.

October 1 - Kansas City wins

Clint Hurdle on the cover of *Sports Illustrated*.

> *If I'd done everything I was supposed to, I would be leading the league in home runs, have the highest batting average, have given $1,000 to the cancer fund and have married Marie Osmond.*
> **Clint Hurdle**

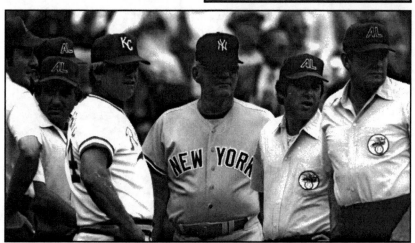

Royals Manager Whitey Herzog and Yankees Manager Bob Lemon meet before Game 1 of the 1978 ALCS.

the regular season finale against Minnesota, 1-0, and finishes with a record of 92-70.

October 3 - ALCS Game 1. For the third straight year, the Royals face the Yankees for the American League pennant. New York raps out 16 hits and easily wins the opener in KC, 7-1.

October 4 - ALCS Game 2. The Royals collect 16 hits and rout the Yankees, 10-4, at Royals Stadium. Gura gets the win.

> *We've got quite a rivalry going here.*
> **Paul Splittorff**
> during the 1978 ALCS

October 6 - ALCS Game 3. George Brett hits three homers off Catfish Hunter at Yankee Stadium, but the Royals still lose, 6-5. Thurman Munson's eighth-inning home run gives the Yanks the win. Doug Bird takes the loss for KC.

October 7 - ALCS Game 4. For the third year in a row the Royals lose the AL pennant to the Yankees. New York wins, 2-1, to take the flag. Leonard loses his second game of the series.

1979

April 5 - The Royals rout the Blue Jays at Royals Stadium on Opening Day, 11-2. Dennis Leonard gets the win.

May 28 - After 16 innings the Royals prevail over the Orioles at Royals Stadium. Larry Gura gets the win in relief.

June 13 - George Scott comes to Kansas City from the Red Sox in exchange for Tom Poquette.

June 15 - After falling behind 11-2, the Royals rally to beat the Brewers, 14-11, at Milwaukee. Willie Wilson becomes the first Royal to hit a homer from both sides of the plate. Steve Mingori gets the win.

August 29 - Royals beat Brewers in KC, 18-8, as Sal Bando and former Royal Buck Martinez pitch.

Willie Wilson

September 21 - U. L. Washington hits a home run from both sides of the plate as the Royals clobber the A's, 13-4.

September 30 - Willie Wilson finishes the season with 83 steals, tops in the American League. The Royals lose the season finale to Oakland, 6-5, and finish the year with an 85-77 record, three games back of the Angels.

October 2 - The Royals fire Manager Whitey Herzog.

Jim Frey

October 24 - Jim Frey is named as the new manager of the Royals.

December 6 - The Royals acquire Willie Aikens and Rance Mulliniks from the Angels for Todd Cruz, Al Cowens and Craig Eaton.

1980

April 10 - Detroit drops the Royals on Opening Day in Kansas City, 5-1. Dennis Leonard takes the loss.

April 30 - Larry Gura pitches a one-hitter for his third shutout in five starts. The Royals win, 3-0.

May 4 - Darrell Porter returns to the starting lineup after spending six weeks in a drug and alcohol rehabilitation center. He drives in three runs in KC's 5-3 win over Boston at Royals Stadium.

May 7 - Kansas City bangs out nine consecutive hits (one short of the AL record set by Boston in 1901) in an eighth-run fourth inning. They beat the White Sox, 8-4, in Chicago.

May 14 - Royals pitchers issue 14 walks in a 16-3 loss to the Yankees.

Dennis Leonard

June 11 - Dennis Leonard pitches a

August 17, 1980 - George Brett stands triumphantly at second base after pushing his batting average above .400.

shutout against the Indians in Cleveland, 5-0. The win is the eighth in a row for the Royals.

August 17 - George Brett goes 4-for-4 against Toronto at Royals Stadium, pushing his season batting average over .400.

August 19 - Brett's 30-game hitting streak comes to an end. He batted .467 with seven game-winning RBIs before being stopped by Jon Matlack of the Texas Rangers at Arlington Stadium. The Royals still win, 4-3.

September 17 - Leonard shuts out Angels in Kansas City, 5-0, as the Royals wrap up the AL West, their fourth title in five years.

September 18 - Willie Wilson steals second and third base in the second inning against the Angels, an AL-record 28th consecutive steal without getting caught. The Royals win, 5-2.

October 4 - Willie Wilson becomes the first player in Major League history to be credited with 700 at-bats in one season. He also sets the mark for the most singles in a season, 183, and becomes only the second player in history to collect 100 hits from each side of the plate. Brett goes 2-for-4 at Royals Stadium to finish the year with a .390 batting average and wins his second AL Batting Championship. Kansas City pounds the Twins, 17-1, as Leonard wins his 20th game of the year.

**The 1980 Kansas City Royals
American League Champions**

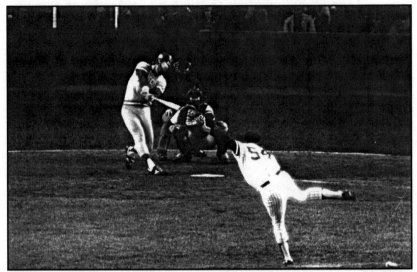

Pennant-winning home run! George Brett hammers a 98 MPH fastball from the Yankees' Goose Gossage for a three-run homer in the top of the seventh inning of Game 3 of the 1980 ALCS. The shot sent the Royals into their first World Series.

October 5 - Paul Splittorff shuts out the Twins, 4-0, and the Royals finish the season with a 97-65 record.

October 8 - ALCS Game 1. For the fourth time in five seasons, the Royals and Yankees meet to determine the AL Champion. Gura pitches a great game and Brett homers at Royals Stadium. Kansas City wins, 7-2.

October 9 - ALCS Game 2. KC takes a 2-games-to-none advantage, winning a squeaker, 3-2. Leonard wins with help from Dan Quisenberry and Brett's relay throw to catch Willie Randolph at the plate late in the game.

> *I'm not even thinking about the World Series. I'll worry about that in another day or two. This day has been too long coming to think about anything else.*
> **Paul Splittorff**
> **on winning the 1980 ALCS**

October 10 - ALCS Game 3. The Royals win the pennant! George Brett's three-run homer off Goose Gossage in the seventh inning gives the Kansas City Royals their first American League Championship and sends them to the team's and city's first World Series. Quisenberry pitches big and gets the win in relief, 4-2.

October 14 - World Series Game 1. The Royals can't hold a four-run lead as the Phillies win an exciting game, 7-6. Aikens homers twice and Leonard takes the loss in Philadelphia.

October 15 - World Series Game 2. Brett is forced out of the game in the 6th inning with a severe case of hemorrhoids. Philadelphia comes from behind again to win, 6-4.

October 16 - Brett has minor surgery for hemorrhoids.

Willie Aikens in the 1980 World Series.

October 17 - World Series Game 3. Willie Aikens' 10th-inning single gives the Royals a 4-3 win in Game 3 for the first World Series triumph in Kansas City's history. Back in the lineup, Brett goes 2-for-4 with a homer.

October 18 - World Series Game 4. Willie Aikens hits two more home runs as the Royals tie the Series at two games apiece, winning 5-3. Dennis Leonard gets the win with relief help from Quisenberry.

October 19 - World Series Game 5. Once again the Phillies stage a rally and win. After giving up two runs in the top of the ninth, the Royals load the bases, only to fall short when Jose Cardenal struck out. Phillies win, 4-3. The series shifts back to Philadelphia with KC down, 3 games to 2.

Jose Cardenal strikes out to end Game 5.

October 21 - World Series Game 6. Steve Carlton pitches the Phillies to the championship, beating the Royals, 4-1. Rich Gale takes the loss for Kansas City.

All my problems are behind me.

George Brett on his hemorrhoids during the 1980 World Series

Mark Stallard

November 18 - George Brett is named the American League MVP for the 1980 season. His .390 batting average was the highest since Ted Williams hit .406 in 1941. Brett added 24 homers and 118 RBIs to go with his impressive batting average.

1981

January 21 - Cesar Geronimo comes to the Royals from Cincinnati in exchange for German Barranca.

April 10 - Kansas City drops the season opener to the Orioles at Baltimore, 5-3. Gura is tagged with the loss.

April 30 - The Royals lose their 10th game against just three wins. Texas beats KC, 7-0, at Royals Stadium.

May 22 - Kansas City's record drops to 9-22 after losing to the Twins, 7-0.

June 12 - The Major League Baseball Players Association goes on strike against Major League owners. Games will not resume until August.

August 10 - The players strike ends and the 1981 "second season" begins. The Royals lose to Baltimore in 12 innings, 3-2.

August 31 - Dick Howser replaces Jim Frey as manager.

October 5 - The Royals shut out the Indians at Cleveland, 9-0, clinching the second-half AL West title. Splittorff records the win. The second game of the scheduled doubleheader is canceled. Because of the strike, a divisional play-off will determine the winner of the AL West. The Royals will meet first-half winner Oakland in a best-of-five series. KC's combined record for the year is 50-53.

Dick Howser

October 6 - Western Division Playoff Game 1. The Royals are shut out at home by Oakland, 4-0. Dennis Leonard loses as KC manages only four hits.

October 7 - Western Division Playoff Game 2. Oakland scores a run in the top of the eighth and hangs on to win, 2-1. The A's lead the series two games to none.

October 9 - Western Division Playoff Game 3. The A's sweep the Royals by winning at Oakland, 4-1, to capture the AL West title.

December 11 - The Royals send Clint Hurdle to the Reds for Scott Brown. In another trade, Rich Gale and Bill Laskey go to the Giants for Jerry Martin.

December 21 - Mike Jones, the Royals' standout rookie pitcher in the 1981 season, crashes his car near Rochester, NY. Jones doesn't pitch again in the majors until 1984 due to injuries sustained in the accident.

John Wathan, George Brett and Mike Jones in the '81 Playoffs.

> *It was the kind of year that you'd like to forget.*
>
> **George Brett**
> on the 1981 season

1982

March 2 - Kansas City picks up Buddy Black from the Mariners for Manny Castillo.

March 24 - Greg Pryor is acquired from the White Sox for Jeff Schattinger.

March 30 - A trade that will have major implications for KC in the next several seasons—Vida Blue and Bob Tufts come to Kansas City from the Giants for Atlee Hammaker, Renie Martin, Brad Wellman, and Craig Chamberlain.

April 5 - The Royals get hammered at Baltimore, 13-5, in the season opener. Dennis Leonard takes the loss.

May 16 - Hal McRae collects the 1,500th base hit of his career.

> *I'm not much on sour grapes. I think of the season only in terms of game 1 through 162—not one incident, one loss, one call or one player move.*
>
> **Dick Howser**
> on the 1982 season

August 3 - Frank White hits for the cycle. The Royals beat the Tigers in Kansas City, 6-5.

August 24 - John Wathan steals his 31st base of the season in the Royals 5-3 win over the Rangers. The theft breaks the single-season record for catchers set by Ray Schalk in 1916. Wathan finishes the season with 36 stolen bases.

October 3 - Willie Wilson wins the American League batting title on the last day of season, finishing with a .332 average. Hal McRae finishes the season with

John Wathan

133 RBIs, tops in the American League. The Royals lose to Oakland, 6-3, and finish the year at 90-72, second in the AL West.

1983

February 4 - The Royals trade Cecil Fielder to the Blue Jays for Leon Roberts.

April 4 - The Royals beat the Orioles, 7-2, in Baltimore to open the season. Larry Gura gets the win.

George Brett lifts one at Royals Stadium.

April 20 - George Brett wallops three home runs and drives in seven runs to lead the Royals to an 8-7 win over Detroit at Tiger Stadium. Quisenberry gets the win in relief.

May 17 - Ewing Kauffman sells 49 percent of the Royals to Memphis businessman Avron Fogelman. At the time, Fogelman agreed to purchase the remaining 51 percent of the team no later than 1991, but instead sold his percentage back to Kauffman in 1991.

Gaylord Perry

June 7 - Kansas City sends Bob Tufts to the Reds for Charlie Leibrandt.

July 6 - The Royals claim future Hall-of-Fame pitcher Gaylord Perry off waivers from the Seattle Mariners.

July 24 - The Royals and Yankees become involved in one of the great controversies in baseball history—the "Pine Tar" game. With two out in the top of the ninth at Yankee Stadium, George Brett hits a two-run homer off Goose Gossage to give the Royals a 5-4 lead. At the request of Yankee manager Billy Martin, home plate umpire Tim McClelland checks Brett's bat and finds pine tar is more than 18 inches from the knob—a rules violation. McClelland calls Brett out, ending the game and giving the Yankees a 4-3 win. Brett goes berserk at the ruling and the Royals protest the game.

The Pine Tar Game made national headlines.

July 27 - The Royals Gaylord Perry records his 3,500th career strikeout; he is the fourth pitcher to attain that mark. The Royals beat Cleveland, 5-4.

I've never been that mad in my whole life.

George Brett
on the Pine Tar Incident

July 28 - American League President Lee MacPhail upholds the Royals' protest of the Pine Tar game. MacPhail finds that Brett's bat was not "altered to improve the distance factor." Brett's home run is allowed and MacPhail orders the game resumed from the point of the dispute—two out in the top of the ninth with the Royals ahead 5-4.

> *I expected something more exciting. It was an ordinary game except for one thing: I didn't give up a hit.*
>
> **Dan Quisenberry**
> on finishing the Pine Tar game

August 5 - Waviers are asked on Vida Blue for the purpose of giving him his unconditional release from the Royals.

August 18 - Pine Tar game conclusion. 1,245 fans turn out at Yankee Stadium to see Hal McRae strike out and pitcher Dan Quisenberry retire the Yankees in order in the bottom of the ninth inning. The Royals win the much protested game, 5-4.

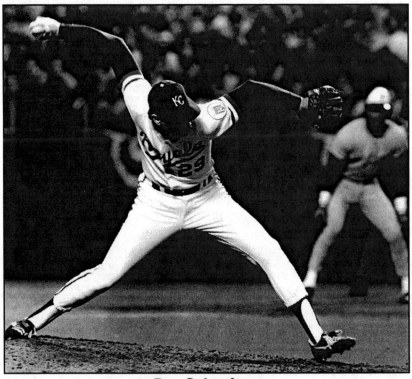

Dan Quisenberry

Pine Boxes

Before the Royals protest was upheld and the Pine Tar Game was ordered to be resumed at the point following George Brett's home run, the box dated July 24, 1983, was the official record of the game. After the replay, the box dated August 18, 1983, became the official box for the game. Although not recorded in the box because it wasn't an official figure, the conclusion of the game attracted only 1,245 fans. Yankee manager Billy Martin was responsible for most of the changes in the box score because of his numerous lineup alterations.

July 24, 1983

Kansas City (3)

	AB	R	H	BI
Wilson, cf	3	0	0	0
Sheridan, cf	2	0	0	0
Washington, ss	5	0	1	0
Brett, 3b	5	0	2	0
McRae, dh	3	0	0	0
Otis, rf	4	0	1	0
Wathan, 1b	3	2	1	0
Roberts, lf	3	0	2	0
Aikens, 1b	1	0	0	0
White, 2b	4	1	2	2
Slaught, c	4	0	3	1
Totals	37	3	12	3

New York (4)

	AB	R	H	BI
Campaneris, 2b	4	1	2	0
Nettles, 3b	3	0	0	0
Piniella, rf	4	1	1	0
Mumphrey, cf	0	0	0	0
Baylor, dh	4	1	1	2
Winfield, cf	4	1	3	2
Kemp, lf	4	0	0	0
Balboni, 1b	2	0	0	0
Mattingly, rf	1	0	0	0
Smalley, ss	3	0	1	0
Cerone, c	2	0	0	0
Totals	31	4	8	4

KANSAS CITY	010	101	000—3
NEW YORK	010	003	00x—4

DP—New York 1. LOB—KC 9, New York 5.
3B—White, Slaught, Baylor, HR—Winfield (16).
GAME-WINNING RBI—Winfield (13).

Kansas City

	IP	H	R	ER	BB	SO
Black (L, 4-4)	6	7	4	4	0	2
Armstrong	2	1	0	0	2	0
New York						
Rawley	5-1/3	10	3	3	2	2
D. Murry (W, 3-1)	3-1/3	2	0	0	0	2
Gossage (S, 12)	1/3	0	0	0	0	0

T—2:40. A—33,944.

August 18, 1983

Kansas City (5)

	AB	R	H	BI
Wilson, cf	3	0	0	0
Sheridan, cf	2	0	0	0
Simpson, lf	0	0	0	0
Washington, ss	5	1	1	0
Brett, 3b	5	1	3	2
Pryor, 3b	0	0	0	0
McRae, dh	4	0	0	0
Otis, rf	4	0	1	0
Wathan, 1b	3	2	1	0
Roberts, lf	3	0	2	0
Aikens, 1b	1	0	0	0
White, 2b	4	1	2	2
Slaught, c	4	0	3	1
Totals	38	5	13	5

New York (4)

	AB	R	H	BI
Campaneris, 2b	4	1	2	0
Griffey, 1b	0	0	0	0
Nettles, 3b	3	0	0	0
Piniella, rf	4	1	1	0
Mumphrey, cf	0	0	0	0
Wynegar, c	0	0	0	0
Baylor, dh	4	1	1	2
Winfield, cf	4	1	3	2
Kemp, lf	4	0	0	0
Balboni, 1b	2	0	0	0
Mattingly, rf	2	0	1	0
Smalley, ss	4	0	1	0
Cerone, c	2	0	0	0
Guidry, cf	0	0	0	0
Gamble, ph	1	0	0	0
Totals	34	4	8	4

KANSAS CITY	010	101	002—5
NEW YORK	010	003	000—4

DP—New York 1. LOB—KC 8, New York 5.
3B—White, Slaught, Baylor, HR—Winfield (16), Brett (20).
GAME-WINNING RBI—Brett (10).

	IP	H	R	ER	BB	SO
Kansas City						
Black	6	7	4	4	0	2
Armstrong (W, 6-6)	2	1	0	0	2	0
Quisenberry (S,33)	1	0	0	0	0	0
New York						
Rawley	5-1/3	10	3	3	2	2
D. Murry	3-1/3	2	1	1	0	2
Gossage (L, 10-4)	0	1	1	1	0	0
Frazier	1/3	0	0	0	0	1

* Pitched to one batter in the ninth.
T—2:52. A—33,944.

August 23 - Amos Otis collects his 2,000th career hit, a single, in Kansas City's 10-2 win over Chicago at Royals Stadium.

September 13 - Dan Quisenberry breaks John Hiller's all-time single-season save record, notching his 39th of the season in the Royals 4-3 win over the Angels.

October 2 - The Royals lose at Oakland, 8-4, ending the season with a 79-83 mark, their worst record since 1974.

October 14 - Kansas City Royals players Willie Wilson, Willie Aikens and Jerry Martin plead guilty to one count of conspiring to attempt to possess cocaine.

December 8 - Steve Balboni comes to Kansas City from the Yankees with Roger Erickson in exchange for Mike Armstrong and Duane Dewey.

December 15 - Royal players Willie Aikens, Willie Wilson and Jerry Martin are suspended for one year by Commissioner Bowie Kuhn. An arbitrator later shortens the suspensions.

December 19 - Amos Otis, after 14 seasons with the Royals, leaves the team a free agent and signs a one-year contract with the Pirates. The Royals continue their house-cleaning by trading Willie Aikens to Toronto for Jorge Orta.

1984

April 3 - The Royals open the season in New York and beat the Yankees, 4-2. Buddy Black wins for KC.

April 19 - Bret Saberhagen wins his first Major League game, beating the Tigers, 5-2.

May 23 - Bud Black pitches a gem as the Royals defeat the White Sox at Royals Stadium, 1-0.

June 25 - Kansas City crushes the A's in Kansas City, 16-0. Gubicza gets the win.

Bret Saberhagen

July 1 - Paul Splittorff retires. His 166 wins in 13 seasons are the most in the history of the club.

August 5 - Charlie Leibrandt shuts out the Tigers in Detroit, 4-0.

September 12 - The Royals beat the Minnesota Twins, 3-2, and Dan Quisenberry—saving the game for Bud Black—becomes the first pitcher in Major League history to record 40 or more saves in two consecutive seasons.

September 28 - The Royals clinch the American League

> *I never blamed anyone else for what I did. The Royals have done a lot for me, and I don't want hem to think about me now. I just want them to have a good season.*
> **Willie Wilson, 1984**

> *I never really thought I would see another playoff in Kansas City. We made so many changes so fast, I had a feeling it was going to be a few years before we came together and could contend.*
> **Frank White**
> after clinching the 1984 AL West

The Royals celebrate winning the 1984 AL West Division title.

West, beating the A's in Oakland, 6-5. Charlie Leibrandt is the winning pitcher for the Royals.

September 30 - Oakland beats Kansas City on the last day of the season, 8-2. The Royals finish with a record of 84-78.

October 2 - ALCS Game 1. The Tigers overpower Kansas City at Royals Stadium and win going away, 8-1. Buddy Black is ineffective as the Royals' starter and takes the loss.

Don Slaught and Bud Black in the '84 ALCS.

October 3 - ALCS Game 2. Bret Saberhagen's pitching performance is brilliant, but when the game moves into extra innings, the Royals are unable to score and lose 5-3 in 11 innings. Detroit's John Grubb delivers a two-run double to win the game for the Tigers. Quisenberry is the losing pitcher, and KC heads to Detroit down two games to none.

October 5 - ALCS Game 3. Despite throwing a three-hitter, Charlie Leibrandt receives no offensive help and the Royals lose, 1-0, and are swept out of the ALCS by the Tigers.

1985

January 7 - U. L. Washington is traded to the Montreal Expos for two minor leaguers.

January 18 - In a key move, the Royals acquire catcher Jim Sundberg from the Milwaukee Brewers in a four-team deal that sends catcher Don Slaught to Texas and pitcher Frank Wills to the Mets. Sundberg provides needed stability behind the plate throughout the 1985 season.

February 22 - Dan Quisenberry, Willie Wilson and Frank White are offered lifetime contracts.

April 8 - Buddy Black and Quisenberry combine for a five-hitter as the Royals defeat the Blue Jays, 2-1, before an opening day crowd of 41,086.

April 30 - Steve Balboni swats a grand slam and Bret Saberhagen throws a five-hitter as the Royals defeat the Indians, 5-1.

May 3 - The Royals turn their first triple play since 1972 but lose to the Yankees, 7-1.

May 17 - The Royals acquire Lonnie Smith from the St. Louis Cardinals for outfielder John Morris. Smith plays a key role in the Royals' fortunes throughout the remainder of the season.

May 18 - Larry Gura is released from the team. His career record with the club stands at 111-78.

June 7 - Steve Balboni hits two home runs in the Royals 6-0 win over the Angels.

June 24 - McRae hits two homers and Motley, Smith and Sundberg hit one each in the Royals' 12-6 win over the Twins.

July 11 - George Brett is elected the starting third baseman on the American League All-Star team for the 10th straight year.

August 24 - Brett drives in four runs as the Royals defeat the Rangers, 8-2.

Steve Balboni

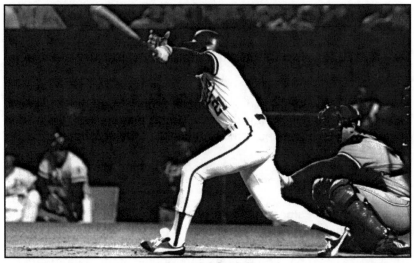

Lonnie Smith

September 6 - The Royals sweep a doubleheader from the Brewers, 4-3 and 7-1. The wins move the team into first place.

September 10 - Hal McRae collects his 2000th career hit, an RBI double, in the Royals' 6-0 win over the Angels.

September 20 - Balboni hits a grand slam, leading the Royals to a 5-1 win over the Twins.

> *Can you believe we won this thing? Look at our stats.*
> **Dane Iorg**
> on winning the 1985 AL West

September 30 - Saberhagen pitches a five-hitter to earn his 20th win of the season, a 3-1 victory over the Angels that moves the Royals into a tie for first place.

October 3 - Danny Jackson defeats the Angels, 4-1, giving the Royals a one-game lead. White, Brett and Balboni homer.

October 5 - The Royals clinch their sixth division title in 10 years, defeating the A's, 5-4. Brett homers for the fifth time in

Danny Jackson

six games and Quisenberry gets the win in relief.

October 6 - Kansas City closes the regular season losing to the A's, 9-3. The team finishes with a record of 91-71.

October 8 - ALCS Game 1. Dave Stieb shuts down the Royals and the Blue Jays win in Toronto, 6-1, to take a one game lead in the series. Leibrandt is the losing pitcher for KC.

October 9 - ALCS Game 2.The Royals lose a tough one, 6-5. After tying the score in the ninth inning and going

Charlie Leibrandt

ahead 5-4 in the 10th, KC gives up two runs to lose. Quisenberry takes the loss as the Royals give up three unearned runs.

October 11 - ALCS Game 3. George Brett plays the game of his life by hitting two homers, a double and single, knocking in three runs and scoring another four to lead the Royals to a 6-5 come-from-behind win. Steve Farr pitches 4-1/3 innings of shutout relief for the win.

Hal McRae congratulates George Brett after one of his two home runs in Game 3 of the 1985 ALCS.

The Royals celebrate winning the 1985 American League Flag.

October 12 - ALCS Game 4. The Royals fall behind three games to one, losing 3-1. Despite pitching well, Leibrandt loses his second game of the series.

October 13 - ALCS Game 5. Danny Jackson tosses a shutout at the Blue Jays, allowing only eight hits to win 2-0. The Royals head back to Toronto down three games to two.

October 15 - ALCS Game 6. Brett leads the way again with another home run as the Royals tie the ALCS, winning 5-3. Hal McRae adds two RBIs and Mark Gubicza records the win. Quisenberry picks up his first save of the series.

> *We're not a dominant club, but we played about as well as you can the last six weeks of the season. We earned this thing.*
>
> **Dick Howser**
> **on the 1985 Royals**

October 16 - ALCS Game 7. Back to the World Series! The Royals complete their improbable comeback by defeating Toronto, 6-2, and win the American League pennant. Jim Sundberg provides the big blow, a bases-loaded triple in the sixth inning. Brett wins the series MVP. The Cardinals await Kansas City in the World Series.

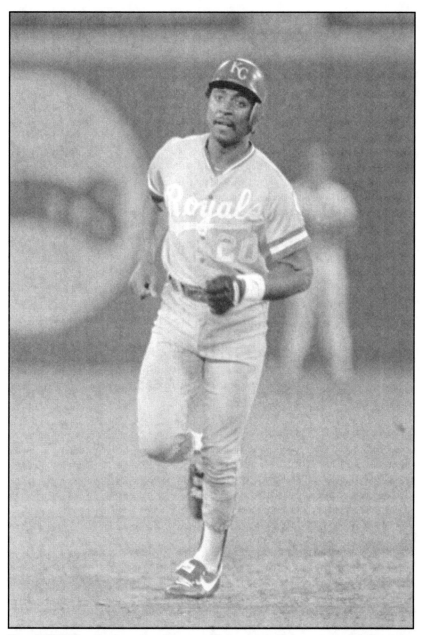

Frank White circles the bases after slugging a two-run homer in Game 3 of the 1985 World Series. The shot led the way to the Royals' 6-1 win.

October 19 - World Series Game 1. Cardinal Pitcher John Tudor controls the Royals and with relief help from Todd Worrell, wins 3-1 at Royals Stadium. Danny Jackson is the losing pitcher.

Brett tags out the Cards' Willie McGee.

October 20 - World Series Game 2. Late-inning heartbreak for Charlie Leibrandt. After limiting the Cardinals to just two hits through eight innings, Charlie gives up 4 runs and loses the game. It is the first time since the 1939 World Series a team comes back from a 2-0 deficit in the ninth inning to win. The teams head to St. Louis with the Cardinals up two games to none.

October 22 - World Series Game 3. Bret Saberhagen limited the Redbirds to six singles and Frank White provides the needed offensive punch with a homer and 3 RBIs. The Royals win the game, 6-1.

October 23 - World Series Game 4. John Tudor is again masterful, limiting Kansas City to five hits and shutting them out, 3-0. The win gives the Cardinals a 3-1 advantage in the Series. Although he pitches well, Buddy Black takes the loss.

October 24 - World Series Game 5. Danny Jackson pitches brilliantly and stops St. Louis. The Royals win, 6-1, sending the Series back to Kansas City.

> *Everything we do not only surprises me but everybody else.*
> **George Brett**
> on Game 6 of 1985 World Series

> *No one in the park was sober.*
> *The sudden emotional surge, from severe communal depression to sudden shared ecstasy, was as intoxicating as rum...People jumped up and down until the stadium shook. Strange men hugged each other and wept with joy...A continuous roar sailed through the air for nearly twenty minutes, until every pair of lungs in the county was too hoarse to contribute any more to it.*
> **Bill James**
> ***The 1986 Bill James Baseball Abstract***
> on the Royals winning Game 6 of the 1985 World Series

Jim Sundberg slides across home plate with the winning run in Game 6 of the 1985 World Series. The Royals' Lonnie Smith looks on as St. Louis catcher Darrell Porter misses the tag.

October 26 - World Series Game 6. The Royals use a controversial call at first base, a couple of Cardinal miscues and solid clutch hitting to rally in the bottom of the ninth inning and win, 2-1, sending the Series to a seventh game. Dane Iorg, batting for Dan Quisenberry, lines a 2-run single to right field to send the Royals home winners and forever put a stamp of what-might-have-been on this game for the Cardinals. Quiz gets the win.

October 27 - World Series Game 7. THE ROYALS WIN THE WORLD SERIES! Bret Saberhagen glides through the St. Louis hitters the entire game, while the Royals explode for 11 runs. After Darryl Motley hits a 2-run homer in the second inning, it's easy cruising for the Royals, who collect 14 hits in the game. Saberhagen wins the World Series MVP.

> *There were times when I thought it would take a miracle for us to win this year, but we never gave up. This is incredible.*
>
> **Jim Sundberg**
> after Game 7 of World Series

November 18 - Bret Saberhagen wins the American League Cy Young Award.

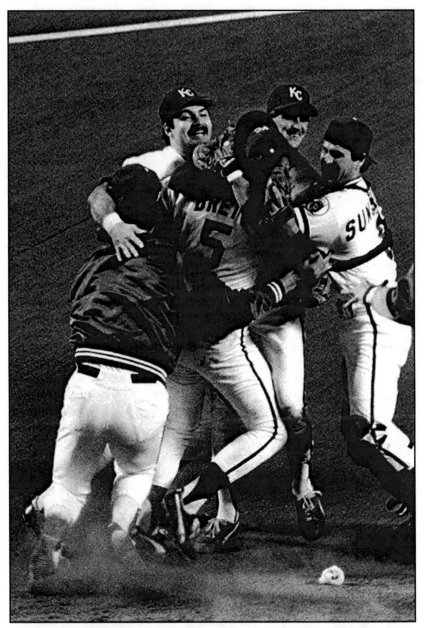

World Champions! Steve Balboni, George Brett, Bret Saberhagen and Jim Sundberg start celebrating following the final out of Game 7 in the 1985 World Series.

The 1985 World Champions

1986

April 1 - Kansas City obtains Angel Salazar from the Mets for Tony Ferreira. Salazar will be the Royals' 1986 Opening Day shortstop.

April 8 - The Royals drop the season opener to the Yankees in New York, 4-3. Buddy Black is the losing pitcher.

April 12 - Pitcher Dennis Leonard pitches a three-hit shutout against Toronto after three years of inactivity due to four different surgeries.

May 25 - George Brett collects his 2,000th career hit off Chicago's Joel Davis in Kansas City's 2-1 win over the White Sox.

June 7 - The Royals pick Bo Jackson in the 4th round of the June draft.

June 8 - David Cone makes his Major League debut with the Royals, giving up three hits and one run in one inning of work.

June 10 - Brett rips five hits against the Mariners at Royals Stadium. Kansas City wins, 9-5.

June 21 - Bo Jackson signs with the Royals.

June 30 - Bo Jackson makes his professional debut with the Memphis Chicks.

The Royals are presented the 1985 World Series trophy at the team's 1986 home opener.

July 8 - The Royals lose to Baltimore in 13 innings at Royals Stadium, 8-4. It's the team's 11th straight loss, a club record.

July 9 - Danny Jackson shuts out the Orioles, 3-0, to end the 11-game losing streak.

July 15 - Dick Howser manages the American League All Star team to a 3-2 win in Houston. Frank White homers for the AL.

July 18 - The Royals announce Howser will miss the rest of the season to undergo treatment for a brain tumor that is later revealed to be malignant. Third base coach Mike Ferraro takes over the managing duties for the rest of the season.

> *Losing Dick (Howser) was an absolute shock....It put some fear in us. You had to wonder if baseball was really that important.*
>
> **Jamie Quirk, 1986**

September 14 - Bo Jackson hits his first major-league home run, a 475-foot blast off Seattle's Mike Moore in a 10-3 win at Royals Stadium.

October 5 - The Royals end the season losing to the A's in Oakland, 6-0. Saberhagen takes the loss. Kansas City finishes with a record of 76-86.

December 10 - The Royals acquire Danny Tartabull and Rick Luecken from the Mariners for Mike Kingery, Scott Bankhead and Steve Shields.

1987

February 23 - Lacking the strength to work, Dick Howser steps down in his bid to return as the Royals' manager. Billy Gardner is named as his replacement.

March 27 - The Royals trade David Cone and Chris Jelic to the Mets for Ed Hearn, Rick Anderson and Mauro Gozzo.

April 6 - The Royals lose to the White Sox on Opening Day at Royals Stadium, 5-4. Danny Jackson suffers the loss.

May 13 - Willie Wilson collects five hits as the Royals win at Baltimore in 12 innings, 8-7.

June 17 - Dick Howser dies at St. Luke's Hospital in Kansas City.

Danny Tartabull

July 3 - The Royals retire Howser's uniform number, 10.

July 14 - Bo Jackson announces that he will play football for the Los Angeles Raiders as a "hobby."

August 2 - Royals rookie Kevin Seitzer goes 6-for-6 with two home runs and seven RBIs, tying the AL record for hits in a nine-inning game. KC handily beats the Red Sox, 13-5.

August 27 - Billy Gardner is fired. John Wathan is named to manage the Royals. The Royals beat Texas, 3-2, on Brett's 10th-inning home run.

> *It was the worst (atmosphere) since I've been playing. I couldn't wait till the season ended.*
>
> **Frank White**
> on the 1987 season

October 4 - The Royals clobber Minnesota in the season finale at home, 10-1. Gubicza gets the win as the Royals finish with a record of 83-79, second in the AL West.

> *The whole traumatic thing about this year was that we could have won it; we could have won the whole thing.*
>
> **Frank White, 1987**

November 6 - Kansas City sends Danny Jackson and Angel Salazar to the Reds for Kurt Stillwell and Ted Power.

1988

February 2 - The Royals obtain Jeff Montgomery from the Reds for Van Snider.

April 4 - Saberhagen gives up three home runs to Toronto's George Bell and the Royals lose the season opener, 5-3, at Royals Stadium.

June 3 - Kansas City trades Buddy Black to the Indians for Pat Tabler.

June 16 - The Royals beat the A's at Oakland, 9-5. It's the team's 13th win in 14 games and pulls them to within 4-1/2 games of first place. Gubicza gets the win.

Kevin Seitzer

July 4 - The Royals release Dan Quisenberry.

September 26 - Mark Gubicza blanks Seattle at Royals Stadium, 5-0, to win his 20th game of the season.

October 2 - Chicago beats the Royals, 5-1, in the last game of the season. Kansas City finishes with a record of 84-77, third in the AL West.

November 30 - The Royals sign free agent catcher Bob Boone.

1989

April 3 - Kansas City drops the season opener to Toronto at Royals Stadium, 4-3. Mark Gubicza is the losing pitcher.

July 11 - Bo Jackson is voted the Most Valuable Player in the All-Star Game at Anaheim. Jackson homers and steals a base as the American League wins, 5-3.

August 24 - The Royals lose to California, 5-0, ending the team's nine-game wins streak.

September 8 - Brett singles for his 2,500th career hit as the Royals beat the Twins, 6-0. Minnesota's Roy Smith is the victimized pitcher.

September 28 - The Royals are shut out for the 18th time this season, losing at California, 2-0.

> *In a lot of ways it was a good year. But for a team which was thinking pennant from day one, it wasn't good enough.*
>
> **John Wathan**
> on the 1989 season

October 1 - Oakland beats the Royals, 4-3, in the season's final game. Kansas City finishes with a mark of 92-70, good for second place in the AL West.

November 15 - Bret Saberhagen wins the American League Cy Young Award for the second time. Saberhagen received 27 of 28 possible first place votes for his 23-6, 2.16 ERA season.

December 12 - Mark Davis signs a four-year multi-million dollar contract with the Royals. The star relief pitcher won the National

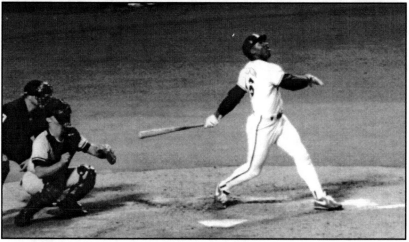

Bo Jackson launches one during action at Royals Stadium.

League Cy Young Award in 1989, making the Royals the first team ever to have both defending winners on the same team.

December 15 - Goodbye Charlie. The Royals trade Charlie Leibrandt and Rick Luecken to the Braves for Gerald Perry and Jim LeMasters.

1990

March 31 - The Royals trade Jose DeJesus to the Phillies for Steve Jeltz.

April 9 - The Royals lose to Baltimore in 11 innings at Royals Stadium, 7-6, to start the season. Jeff Montgomery is pinned with the defeat.

April 14 - The Royals beat Toronto, 3-1, with Saberhagen getting the win and Mark Davis the save. It is the first time ever that two reigning Cy Young Award winners have figured in the same victory.

June 13 - Willie Wilson steals his 600th career base in the Royals' 11-4 win over the Angels.

July 17 - Great news, bad news. Bo Jackson homers three times at Yankee Stadium off Andy Hawkins, but suffers minor tissue damage to his shoulder diving for a ball in the outfield. The injury causes him to miss more than a month of playing time.

Willie Wilson

July 25 - For the second time in his career, George Brett hits for the cycle. The Royals defeat Toronto, 6-1.

August 26 - In his first game after six weeks on the DL, Bo Jackson homers in his first at bat to tie a Major League record with four consecutive homers. KC wins at home over Seattle, 8-2.

October 3 - Brett wins his third batting title, finishing the season with a batting average of .329. He is the first player in Major League history to win three batting titles in three different decades. The Royals still lose at Cleveland in the season's last game, 5-2. The team's final record is 75-86.

October 10 - Herk Robinson is named as the Royals new General Manager.

November 21 - KC signs free-agent pitcher Mike Boddicker to a three-year contract.

> *We just screwed it up from the beginning (of the season). From beginning to end.*
>
> **Bo Jackson**
> on the 1990 season

December 1 - The Royals sign free-agent outfielder/DH Kirk Gibson.

1991

January - Ewing Kauffman buys back Avron Fogelman's 49 percent of the team, and is again sole owner of the club.

March 15 - The Royals release Bo Jackson. After injuring his hip while playing football, it appears his career is over. KC pays a termination fee for his contract. When placed on waivers, all Major League teams pass on Jackson.

April 8 - The Royals win on Opening Day, beating the Indians at Royals Stadium, 4-2. Saberhagen is the winning pitcher.

May 22 - John Wathan is fired. Hal McRae is named to replace him as the Royals' manager.

Kirk Gibson

May 24 - Hal McRae loses his managerial debut, 3-2, at Minnesota.

June 6 - The Royals win the longest game in team history, 4-3, against the Rangers at Royals Stadium. Mike Boddicker gets the 18-inning win after 6 hours and 28 minutes.

Bret Saberhagen

July 6 - Danny Tartabull hits three homers against the A's, the only Royals player to do so at Royals Stadium. The A's still win, 9-7.

July 17 - The Royals win another long game, this time a 15-inning affair, dropping Baltimore at home, 9-8.

August 26 - Bret Saberhagen throws a no-hitter against Chicago at Royals Stadium, striking out five and walking two in the 7-0 win.

> *This is something I'll remember forever. But truthfully, you have to give credit to everyone behind me. Any you have to have some luck to do this.*
>
> **Bret Saberhagen, 1991**
> **after his no-hitter**

October 6 - Kansas City loses the last game of the season at California, 3-1. Mark Davis is the loser, and the team finishes with a record of 82-80.

December 9 - The Royals sign free-agent first baseman Wally Joyner.

December 11 - Bombshell trade. Kansas City parts with Bret Saberhagen, sending him and Bill Pecota to the Mets for Gregg Jefferies, Keith Miller and Kevin McReynolds. In other deals, the team also unloads Storm Davis and Todd Benzinger.

1992

January 6 - Danny Tartabull leaves the Royals, signing a contract with the Yankees.

March 10 - The Royals trade Kirk Gibson to the Pirates for Neal Heaton.

April 6 - Kansas City drops the season opener at Oakland, 5-3.

July 21 - Free agent disappointment. After 2-1/2 years of poor performances, KC unloads Mark Davis to the Braves for Juan Berenguer.

August 29 - Kansas City sends Sean Berry and Archie Corbin to the Expos for Chris Haney and Bill Sampen.

September 30 - 3,000 hits! George Brett goes 4-for-5 at Anaheim, giving him 3,000 major-league hits for his career. The 3,000th hit comes off the Angels' Tim Fortugno. The Royals win, 4-0.

> *It happened so quick, I really didn't have time to prepare myself for it... But I'm relieved, very relieved.*
>
> **George Brett, 1992**
> after getting his 3,000th hit

October 4 - The Royals lose at home to the Twins in the last game of the year, 6-0. The team finishes at 72-90, the worst record since 1970.

November 19 - The Royals trade Dennis Moeller and Joel Johnston to the Pirates for second baseman Jose Lind.

December 8 - The Royals sign free-agent David Cone to a three-year, $18 million contract, making him the game's highest-paid pitcher. The Royals also sign free agent shortstop Greg Gagne.

1993

February 12 - Gregg Jeffries and Ed Gerald are sent to St. Louis for Felix Jose and Craig Wilson.

April 5 - The Red Sox spoil the home opener for the Royals, winning 3-1. Roger Clemens is the winner for Boston, Appier takes the loss.

May 13 - Brett hits the 300th home run of his career at Cleveland Stadium off the Indians' Mark Clark. The Royals win the game, 7-3.

June 19 - Kansas City signs free agent third baseman Gary Gaetti.

Greg Gagne

July 2 - Royals Stadium officially becomes Kauffman Stadium.

August 1 - Royals owner Ewing Kauffman dies at the age of 76.

> *The game became a job. It wasn't a game anymore. And baseball shouldn't be treated that way.*
>
> **George Brett, 1993**

September 29 - Brett singles in his final at bat at Kauffman Stadium. Kansas City beats Cleveland, 3-2.

October 3 - The Royals finish the season at Texas and win, 4-1. It is also Brett's final game as a Royal. Jeff Montgomery posts his 45th save, tops in the AL, as well as tying Dan Quisenberry for the all-time Royals mark. Finally, Kevin Appier becomes the second Royal ever to win the AL's ERA crown, posting a 2.56 mark. The team finishes with an 84-78 mark, good for third place in the AL West.

1994

January 5 - Kevin McReynolds is unloaded on the Mets for Vince Coleman.

April 4 - The Royals open the season at Baltimore and lose, 6-3. Appier is the losing pitcher for KC.

May 14 - George Brett's No. 5 is retired and he is inducted into the Royals Hall of Fame.

July 16 - Wally Joyner collects five hits against the Tigers at Kauffman Stadium, but the Royals still lose, 13-7.

July 23 - David Cone beats the Tigers in Detroit, 4-1. It is the first win in what becomes a 14-game winning streak.

August 6 - The streak is over. The Royals' 14-game winning streak is halted by the Seattle Mariners in a game moved to Kauffman Stadium, on short notice, due to structural damage at Seattle's Kingdome. The Mariners win big, 11-2, as Gubicza takes the loss.

Wally Joyner

August 10 - The Royals lose at California, 2-1, and the baseball season ends the next day because of the players' strike.

> *I try to put myself in the shoes of the fans. I come up with the same question, 'What are we going to give back to the fan?'*
>
> **David Cone, 1994 on the players' strike**

September 14 - The rest of the 1994 season, including the World Series, is officially canceled. Kansas City finishes with a record of 64-51, third in the AL Central.

October 7 - Hal McRae is fired as the Royals manager and replaced by Bob Boone.

Winter - David Cone becomes the second Royals pitcher to win the American League Cy Young Award. Bob Hamelin wins the American League Rookie of the Year Award. The artificial turf at Kauffman Stadium is ripped up and replaced with grass. Also, the fences from left center field to right center field are moved in 10 feet.

Bob Hamelin

1995

March 17 - Muriel Kauffman passes away.

April 2 - The players strike, which lasted 234 days and caused the cancellation of the 1994 World Series, ends as the owners accept the players' offer to return.

April 5 - Brian McRae is traded to the Cubs for Derek Wallace and Geno Morones.

April 6 - For the second time in his career, David Cone is traded from the Royals. This time KC sends him to Toronto for Chris Stynes, David Sinnes and Tony Medrano.

David Cone

April 26 - Opening Day. Kauffman Stadium has a grass field for the first time. The Royals beat the Orioles, 5-1, with Appier getting the win.

April 29 - John Nunnally leads off the game against the Yankees with a home run, becoming the 70th player—and first member of the Royals—to homer in his first at bat. The Royals lose, 10-3, at Kauffman Stadium.

June 16 - The Royals extend their win-streak to seven games with a 3-1, 13-inning win over Oakland. Jeff Montgomery pitches a perfect 13th inning to pick up the save.

June 21 - Montgomery notches his 200th career save against the Angels in California. The Royals win, 6-3.

> *I love the four-day rotation. The more I can pitch, the better.*
>
> **Kevin Appier, 1995**

July 2 - The Royals retire Frank White's No. 20 and induct him into the Royals Hall of Fame. KC loses to the White Sox, 6-5, in 10 innings.

July 30 - The Royals wear replicas of the 1924 Kansas City Monarchs uniforms during their game with the Tigers at Kauffman Stadium. The Tigers wear 1920 Detroit Stars uniforms as the two team commemorate Negro League baseball. Kansas City wins, 3-2, and Montgomery gets the save.

August 15 - The Royals trade Vince Coleman to Seattle for a player to be named later.

September 1 - The Royals defeat the Rangers, 5-2, for their sixth win in a row. It is also the team's eighth win in their last nine games and gives them a lead in the American League wild card race. Gordon gets the win against Texas.

> *We've got to get our act together. We have to have a gut-check and know what's in front of us. We've played well all year and then, right by the All-Star break, we couldn't find ourselves.*
>
> **Tom Gordon, 1995**

September 23 - Kansas City loses their sixth game in a row to Cleveland, 7-3. The loss virtually eliminates the team from the AL wild card race. Tom Gordon takes the loss.

October 1 - The Royals get hammered by Cleveland in the last game of the year, 17-7. They finish with a mark of 70-74, which is surprisingly good enough for 2nd place in the AL Central.

We didn't mean to play it that way. We have had a lot of trouble scoring points.

Bob Boone, 1995
after getting swept by the A's

December 9 - After spending the 1995 season with the Red Sox, catcher Mike MacFarlane returns to Kansas City, signing as a free agent with the Royals.

December 17 - Jose Offerman comes to the Royals from Los Angeles in exchange for pitcher Billy Brewer.

December 21 - The Royals trade Wally Joyner to San Diego for infielder-outfielder Bip Roberts. Tom Gordon leaves Kansas City, opting to sign a three-year deal with the Red Sox.

Winter - Gary Gaetti leaves the Royals, signing with St. Louis. Greg Gagne also opts for free agency and inks a deal with the Los Angeles Dodgers.

1996

February 1 - The Royals sign free-agent pitcher Tim Belcher to a one-year contract.

April 2 - Kansas City loses the season opener in Baltimore, 4-2. Appier takes the loss.

April 3 - Kansas City turns a triple play on the Orioles but still lose, 7-1. Gubicza is KC's losing pitcher.

April 13 - Despite getting only one hit, Kansas City beats the Brewers in Milwaukee, 3-2. Michael Tucker follows a pair of walks with a three-run homer for the game winner. Gubicza gets the win.

May 12 - The Royals steal six bases against the Mariners but lose anyway, 8-5.

May 24 - Mark Gubicza wins his last game as a Royal, pitching a

He already is going to punch me in the mouth if he doesn't pitch on Saturday.

Bob Boone, 1996
joking about Appier's reaction if he has to miss a start

shutout against the Rangers at Kauffman Stadium, 8-0.

June 1 - Jeff Montgomery makes his 500th appearance for the Royals. He also takes the loss for the game as Kansas City loses to the Blue Jays, 5-3, in 10 innings.

July 20 - Jeff Montgomery saves the 239th game of his career to pass Dan Quisenberry and set a new Royals team record. Kansas City beats the White Sox in Chicago, 7-5.

August 10 - Johnny Damon belts a grand slam off California's Jim Abbott. The Royals pound the Angels, 18-3.

Jeff Montgomery

August 24 - As they did the year before, the Royals and Tigers wear the uniforms of the Detroit Stars and Kansas City Monarchs. The Royals win the game, 9-2.

September 29 - The Royals end the season with a win against Cleveland at home, 4-1. Belcher earns his 15th win of the season. Kansas City finishes with a 75-86 record, and is the first Royals team in the club's history to end the season in last place.

October 28 - After 13 seasons in Royal blue, Mark Gubicza is traded to the Angels for DH Chili Davis.

December 13 - Kansas City acquires Jay Bell and Jeff King from Pittsburgh in exchange for Joe Randa, Jeff Granger, Jeff Wallace and Jeff Martin.

1997

January 28 - Kansas City acquires Yamil Benitez from the Expos for Melvin Bunch.

March 26 - The Royals place DH-1B Bob Hamelin, the 1994 American League Rookie of the Year, on waivers for the purpose of giving him his unconditional release.

April 2 - Kansas City drops the season opener in Baltimore, 4-2. Jamie Walker takes the loss in relief.

> *If he can't find me a reliever, then I can't win*
>
> **Bob Boone, 1997**
> on Royals GM Herk Robinson

April 7 - The numbers of George Brett (5), the late Dick Howser (10) and Frank White (20) are officially retired before the game and permanently displayed at the bottom of the Kauffman Stadium scoreboard. The Royals add to the festivities by winning their home opener over the Orioles, 6-5.

June 7 - Chili Davis homers from both sides of the plate against Texas at Kauffman Stadium, the 10th time in his 16-year career the veteran DH has accomplished the feat. He is the third Royal to turn the trick.

Kevin Appier

June 13 - The Royals play in their first inter-league game at Pittsburgh, losing to the Pirates, 5-3.

June 18 - Jeff King slams a grand slam as the Royals beat the Astros in Houston, 6-2.

July 8 - Bob Boone is fired as the Royals manager. Tony Muser is named the club's new manager.

July 10 - Kansas City drops Muser's managerial debut to the White Sox at home, 6-3.

July 12 - The Royals honor Jackie Robinson in pregame ceremonies and unveil a permanent display of his signature and, along with all of baseball, retire his jersey number 42 at the base of the jumbotron screen behind left

Mike MacFarlane

field. Tom Goodwin will be allowed to continue wearing number 42.

July 13 - The Royals lose for the 12th straight time, a new club record. The White Sox outlast KC at Kauffman Stadium, 7-6.

July 25 - Kansas City trades outfielder Tom Goodwin to the Texas Rangers for third baseman Dean Palmer.

August 12 - Jeff Montgomery becomes the 12th major leaguer to accumulate 250 career saves. The Royals beat the Yankees in New York, 6-4.

Jeff King

August 29 - The Royals and Cardinals play for the first time since the 1985 World Series. The Cardinals win at Kauffman Stadium, 9-7.

August 30 - Five different Royals hit home runs as the Royals clobber the Cardinals in the second game of their inter-league series, 16-5. A brawl erupts in the fourth inning after St. Louis pitcher Mark Petkovsek hits Kansas City's Johnny Damon with a pitch and Damon charges the mound. Petkovsek had just given up a grand slam to Jermaine Dye, giving the Royals a 14-1 lead. Both benches and bullpens empty onto the field.

August 31 - Bip Roberts is traded to the Cleveland Indians for right-handed minor league pitcher Roland de la Maza.

September 27 - The Royals finish the season with a win at Chicago, beating the White Sox, 10-4. Ricky Bones gets the win as Kansas City finishes in last place in the AL Central for the second straight year with a record of 67-93.

September 30 - Royals first baseman Jeff King is tabbed American League Player of the Week. King hit four home

Johnny Damon

runs and knocked in 14 runs in the final week of the season.

It's been my dream for about 30 years to have an opportunity to take a team and make it better. I'd had eight interviews. But it was like I'd had eight at-bats and never hit the ball out of the infield. I hope I spend the rest of my baseball career in Kansas City.

Tony Muser, 1997

November 1 - After weeks of speculation about a possible move to the National League as part of Major League Baseball's realignment process, it is announced that the Royals will remain in the American League, staying in the Central Division.

November 20 - Jeff Conine, taken by the Florida Marlins when the Royals left him unprotected in the 1992 expansion draft, is traded back to Kansas City for minor-league pitcher Blaine Mull.

December 22 - Free-agent DH Hal Morris signs with the Royals.

1998

January 20 - The Royals sign veteran infielder Terry Pendleton and Lee Smith, all-time leader in saves, to minor league contracts. Pendleton makes the club, but Smith retires when he is asked to start the season at Omaha.

March 31 - Kansas City opens the season in Baltimore and wins, 4-1. Tim Belcher pitches well and gets the win. Jeff Montgomery picks up the save.

April 7 - Baltimore spoils the home opener, easily beating the Royals at Kauffman Stadium, 11-7. Glendon Rusch takes the loss.

April 8 - The Royals send catcher Mike Macfarlane to Oakland for outfielder Shane Mack.

May 23 - The Royals lose to the Rangers in Texas, 7-3, the team's eighth straight loss. Glendon Rusch is the loser for Kansas City.

Dean Palmer

Tony Muser

June 2 - In the process of losing to the Angels at Kauffman Stadium, six Royals are ejected as the result of an out-of-control beanball war: Manager Tony Muser, Jim Pittsley, coach Rich Dauer, coach Jamie Quirk, Scott Service and for taking a cheap shot at Angels Frank Bolick in the ninth inning brawl, Felix Martinez, who wasn't in the lineup. The Angels also suffer six ejections, but they prevail in the game, 7-5. Chris Haney is the losing pitcher for KC.

> *I've got to serve my time. It's going to have to be done. I'll take my medicine like a man and do it.*
> **Tony Muser, 1998**
> **on serving his**
> **eight-game suspension**

June 3 - Rookie shortstop Felix Martinez is sent to Omaha.

June 30 - The Royals defeat the Cardinals in St. Louis, 6-1. Cardinal Mark McGwire slams one of his record 70 home runs in the game, but the Royals don't give up anything else. Glendon Rusch picks up the win for Kansas City.

August 1 - The Royals steal a team record eight bases against the Orioles at Kauffman Stadium and win, 9-5. Jose Offerman leads the way with four steals.

> *I got an opportunity to run and we just did it. It's part of our game. Today was a good day for us.*
>
> **Jose Offerman, 1998**
> on the Royals eight stolen base
> against the Orioles

August 20 - The Royals Board of Directors announces New York attorney Miles Prentice and his group has the best bid to purchase the franchise, but that they are also lacking the required amount of local owners.

> *I think we'll get it done. I love baseball. I'm still having fun. This has been an interesting odyssey*
>
> **Miles Prentice, 1998**
> on buying the Royals

September 24 - Jeff Montgomery notches his 36th save of the season as the Royals win, 6-4. Jose Rosado gets the club's final win of the year against the White Sox at Kauffman Stadium.

September 27 - Kansas City closes the season with a 7-6 loss to the White Sox. Tim Belcher is the loser for the Royals. The team finishes the season with a 72-89 record and third place finish in the AL Central.

September 30 - Dan Quisenberry loses his battle with brain cancer and passes away at his home. He was 45 years old.

November 4 - The Royals announce that radio broadcaster Fred White would not return for the 1999 season. White had been a part of the Royals broadcast team for 25 years.

November 13 - Miles Prentice and his group is formally selected by the Royals Board of Directors as the successful bidder for purchasing the Royals. Prominent members of the Prentice Group include Crosby Kemper, Buck O'Neil, Tom Watson, James B. Nutter, Jr., and Nancy Kauffman—Ewing and Muriel's daughter-in-law.

Tim Belcher

December 7 - Jeff Montgomery, the Royals career saves leader, agrees to a one-year contract worth 2.5 million dollars.

December 10 - Kansas City sends former first-round pick Juan LeBron to the Mets for third baseman and former Royal Joe Randa. The club also signs free agent shortstop Rey Sanchez.

> *It wasn't about money, but it was about a principle that revolved around money.*
>
> **Jeff Montgomery, 1998**
> **on his new contract with KC**

> *We finished third in a weak division other than Cleveland. We have a lot of work to do to compete in this division.*
>
> **Tony Muser, 1998**

December 14 - The Royals sign free-agent catcher Chad Kreuter, formerly with the Angels, to a one-year contract.

December 21 - Free-agent pitcher Alvin Morman, formerly with the Giants, signs a one-year contract with the Royals.

1999

January 5 - George Brett is selected for induction into the National Baseball Hall of Fame in Cooperstown, New York. The induction ceremony will be held July 25, 1999. Nolan Ryan and Robin Yount will join Brett in the Hall of Fame.

January 14 - Kansas City re-signs pitcher Scott Service to a one-year contract.

Royals Players Trivia

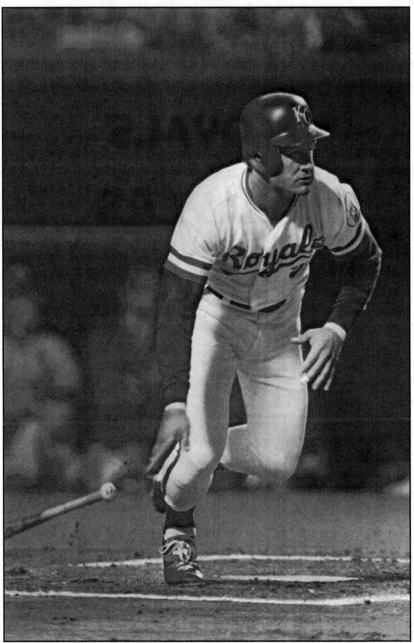

George Brett

George Brett

I have never seen a player who could dominate a baseball game, or a series, or a month of series, the way that George Brett can dominate. Brett is an amazing hitter—strong, with tremendous bat control, excellent command of the strike zone. His swing is a thing of beauty.

Bill James, 1988
The Bill James Historical Baseball Abstract

If you saw him play, then you know how extraordinarily remarkable his baseball talents were. Running, fielding, throwing and most of all, hitting. His career was filled with clutch hits, pennant-winning home runs and amazing batting exhibitions that covered long stretches of time. George Brett was a great baseball player, and with his induction ceremony on July 25, 1999, in Cooperstown, New York, a most deserving Hall-of-Famer.

Brett helped make the Royals champions, not just with his hitting (which was enough to make most teams champions), but also with his heart, spirit and competitive nature. His greatest season was 1985 when he stormed through the final two weeks of the season, literally carrying the Royals on his back as he led them to the division title, American League pennant, and then to the world championship.

Brett's career accomplishments, the number of hits, RBIs, HRs, etc., are overwhelming, but he was more than statistics. Brett was the game-winning hit, the double to left-center, and even the Gold Glove at third.

He was, and always will be, Kansas City's favorite baseball player.

1. Where did Brett go to high school?

2. Brett got his first Major League hit off of which White Sox pitcher on August 2, 1973?

3. Who gave up Brett's first Major League home run?

4. How many times did Brett lead the American League in triples?

5. How many times did Brett lead the American League in doubles?

6. Brett twice collected 200 or more hits in a single season. What two years were they?

7. What season did Brett switch to first base?

8. Who gave up Brett's 2,000th hit?

9. Who gave up Brett's 3,000th hit, and when and where did he get it?

10. What happened after he got the 3,000th hit?

11. How many pinch-hit home runs did Brett hit for the Royals?

12. Who was the Texas pitcher that ended Brett's 30-game hitting streak in 1980?

13. In which stadium did Brett collect his 1,500th hit?

14. Brett joined an exclusive group when he hit his 300th career home run, being one of six players to hit 300 home runs and have 3,000 hits. Who was the pitcher that gave up Brett's 300th home run?

15. Who are the other five players that accomplished the 300-3,000 feat?

16. Who gave up Brett's 200th home run in 1986?

17. In 1975 George collected 11 consecutive hits off this California pitcher, and ended the season 12 of 14 against him. Who was the pitcher?

18. How many consecutive All-Star teams was George selected to?

19. How many consecutive All-Star Games was George selected to start?

20. How many times did Brett steal home in his career?

21. George's brother Ken played with the Royals for parts of two seasons. What seasons were they?

22. How many hits did George have when he retired?

23. Who gave up George's last hit, and where did he get it?

24. How many games did Brett play in?

25. What is Brett's career batting average?

26. Who are the other two players chosen by the Baseball Writers to go into the Hall of Fame with Brett?

Hal McRae

Charlie Lau means one hundred grand.

Hal McRae, 1976
on what Hitting Coach Charlie Lau
meant to him

It was my biggest disappointment in baseball. We should have won the World Series that year, and everybody in baseball knew it.

Hal McRae
on the 1977 Royals

The ultimate when it comes to designated hitters. Hal set the parameters for the special hitting role, not just in Kansas City, but in all of Major League Baseball. When he became the Royals DH, the team became a consistent winner.

Hard-hitting, hard-nosed and hard playing, Hal never held back throughout his career. He was almost singlehandedly responsible for the new slide rule at second base (still known today as the "McRae rule") that keeps sliding runners at the bag, not the second baseman or shortstop. His teammates called him "Mr. Ribbie" for his penchant to knock in big runs; the Royals Stadium scoreboard called his at bats "Big Mac Attacks."

Hal's managerial career with the Royals shouldn't have ended the way it did, especially since he was a winner at that, too. McRae was named to three All-Star squads during his career, but he'll always be considered an All-Star in Kansas City.

1. Hal played baseball at what university?

2. When and with what team did Hal make his Major League debut?

3. Hal led the American League in doubles twice. What years did he lead and how many did he hit?

4. How many times did Hal lead the AL in RBI?

5. How many career hits does Hal have?

Hal McRae

6. What pitcher was traded with Hal from the Reds to the Royals, and what two Royals players were involved in the trade?

7. What position did Hal hold with the Royals in 1987?

8. Hal lost the batting title to George Brett on the last day of the season in 1976 by .001 points. What was Hal's average?

9. How many times in his career did Hal hit .300 or better?

10. Hal played in four different World Series. How many home runs did he hit in the Fall Classic?

11. What was his batting average in the 1985 World Series?

12. What is his lifetime World Series batting average?

Mark Stallard

Frank White

If any one player in the American League owned a position defensively throughout the 1970's and 1980's, it was Frank White at second base. Kansas City's hometown product set the standard at his position, collecting Gold Gloves as easily as he collected ground balls. Overlooked for offensive output early in his career, Frank powered up and became an important offensive force in the Royals lineup the last half of his career.

The most successful graduate of the Royals' Baseball Academy, Frank led the league in fielding percentage three times, played 62 straight games without an error in 1977, and hit 22 home runs two years in row, 1985-86. But like Brett, Frank was more than statistics. His worth to the team, and Kansas City, extended past the boundaries of the playing field.

Frank returned to Kansas City as the Royals' first base coach in 1997.

1. When and where did Frank White play in his first game for the KC?

2. What position did he play in his first game?

3. When did he get his first hit?

4. When did he play his first game at second base?

5. When and off whom did he hit his first home run?

6. How many Gold Gloves did Frank won?

7. When did Frank win his first Gold Glove?

8. How many Gold Gloves did Frank win in a row?

9. What year was he named to his first AL All-Star game?

10. How many All-Star games was he selected for?

11. Frank earned a starting role in only one All-Star game. What was the year?

12. How many career hits does Frank have?

Frank White

Willie Wilson

The fastest of all Royals? Probably, and then some. As the Royals top pick in the 1974 June Free Agent Draft, Wilson signed with Kansas City, passing on a college scholarship to play football at the University of Maryland.

Willie used his speed well, but he was more than just a runner. His defensive ability in the outfield was not only exciting, but also earned him a Gold Glove; his hitting earned him an American League batting championship. His talents were many, but he'll always be remembered as a base stealer, and that's okay. Remember also his knack for getting on base, hitting inside-the-park home runs, and thrilling Kansas City fans with a level of play matched by few who have worn the Royals uniform.

1. When did Willie play in his first game for the Royals?

2. How many times did Willie lead the AL in stolen bases?

3. Willie holds the Royals team record for triples in a season. How many, and in what year did he set this record?

4. Willie was the second player ever to collect 100 hits from both sides of the plate (batting both right-handed and left-handed) during a season. Who was the first player to accomplish this?

5. In the 1980 season Willie was the first Major Leaguer ever to accomplish this feat. What was it?

6. How many times did Willie lead the American League in Triples?

7. How many times did Willie lead the AL in runs scored?

8. How many batting titles did Willie win?

9. How many All-Star games was Willie selected for?

10. How many stolen bases did Willie collect in the 1985 World Series?

11. What two teams did Willie play for after he left the Royals?

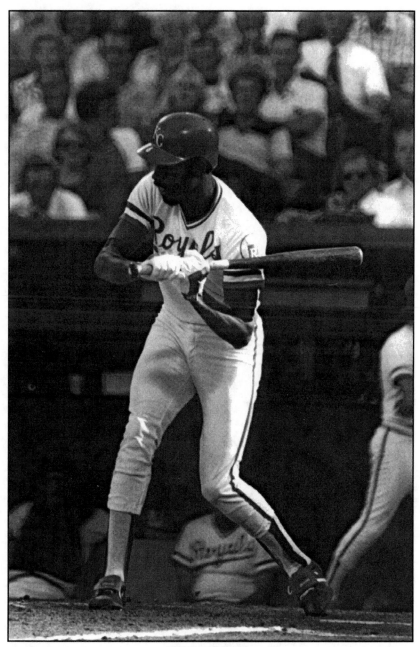

Willie Wilson

Bret Saberhagen

The greatest Royals pitcher of all time? If you're picking one, it has to be Saberhagen. The two-time Cy Young Award winner showed Kansas City fans some of the finest pitching in the American League from 1984-91.

Bret loved pressure games for the Royals. The bigger the game, the better he pitched. In the pennant race, ALCS, or World Series, Saberhagen delivered. A two-time All-Star selection for the American League squad, Bret fought through a couple of disappointing seasons and seemed destined to play out his career in KC, much like Splittorff and Leonard. His unexpected trade and departure from Kansas City still sits uneasy with many fans.

1. Where did Saberhagen attend high school?

2. True or false: Saberhagen pitched a no-hitter in the Los Angeles city high school championship game.

Saberhagen pitches during Game 3 of the 1985 World Series.

3. What position was Saberhagen originally drafted to play?

4. What round was he drafted in?

5. When and against whom did Saberhagen make his Major League debut?

6. How old was he in his debut game?

7. He earned his first start and victory against what team?

8. What team did the Royals trade Saberhagen to and for what players?

9. How many games did Saberhagen win in the 1985 World Series?

10. How many games did Saberhagen win in his career with the Royals?

11. True or False: In addition to the Cy Young Award, Saberhagen also won a Gold Glove in 1989.

12. When and against what team did Saberhagen pitch his no-hitter?

Bo Jackson

Baseball player playing football, or football player pretending to play baseball? Regardless of his talent, expertise and speed, Bo Jackson knew how to create excitement. Whether he was sending an opposing pitcher's fastball to the back end of the bullpen at Royals Stadium or viciously striking out and then snapping the bat across his leg like a twig, Bo knew baseball. Forget about the football "hobby" and the career-ending hip injury. Bo gave Kansas City something they'd never had before, a media superstar. Most of the praise he received was deserved, most of the criticism was not.

His shooting-star career was highly scrutinized and, in the end, lamented. He wasn't in the game—at least wearing a Royals uniform—long enough. His presence on the field is missed, maybe more so by the media than the fans. His combination of power and speed might have eventually eclipsed all power-speed records, but even in his brief time (four full seasons with KC), his talent, like George Brett's, made fans feel the Royals always had a chance to win.

1. Who gave up Bo Jackson's first Major League hit on September 2, 1986?

2. Which Seattle pitcher gave up Jackson's first Major League home run? When and where did Bo hit it?

3. During his career at Kansas City, Bo only once led the American League in a hitting category. What was the category, how many and what year?

4. Did Bo ever win a Gold Glove? If so, when?

5. In 1988, Bo became the first Royal ever to accomplish this feat of speed and power in the same season. He repeated it in 1989. What did he do?

6. In what year did Bo win college football's Heisman Trophy?

7. What was Bo's uniform number when he played for the Los Angeles Raiders?

Bo Jackson

8. Bo homered in four consecutive at bats in 1990. Who was the pitcher that gave up the fourth home run?

9. What year did Bo win the All-Star Game MVP?

10. Which National League pitcher gave up a home run to Bo in that All-Star game?

11. Bo joined Willie Mays as the only other player ever to do these two things in an All-Star game. What are they?

Larry Gura

When Larry Gura joined the Royals in the middle of the 1976 season, it was impossible to know the kind of impact he was going to have on the future success of the team. From his pennant-saving performance against Oakland at the end of the '76 season to his brilliant pitching in the 1980 World Series, Larry provided outstanding lefthanded stuff on the Royals staff for more than nine seasons. That he ended his career as fourth in all-time wins on the club with 111 is not only a tribute to his effectiveness as a pitcher, but also his ability just to win games.

1. Larry was an All-American pitcher at what university?

2. What team did Larry defeat twice in the College World Series to help lead his school to the national title?

3. What two Major League teams did Gura play for before joining the Royals?

4. Who did the Royals trade to acquire Larry?

5. What was Gura's highest win total in one season?

6. What team did he finish his career with?

7. How many games did Gura win in the 1980 World Series?

8. How many All-Star games was he selected for?

9. What was Gura's ERA for the 1980 World Series?

10. Larry posted a career high for saves with 10 in 1977. What was his second-highest season total after that?

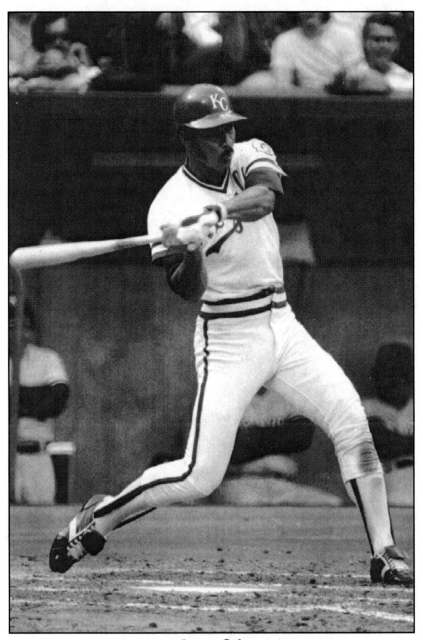

Amos Otis

Amos Otis

The Royals first real superstar, Otis came to Kansas City (he was stolen, really, for the Mets didn't know what they had) and filled the spaces of center field with grace, speed and Gold Glove defensive skill. He always played deep, possessing an uncanny knack for coming in on a ball to make the play. Otis added speed and average at the plate, and peppered the opposing teams with occasional power. He led the American League in doubles twice with 36 in 1970 and 40 in 1976. He tied an American League record by stealing seven bases in two consecutive games in 1975, and finished his career with 341 steals.

Always a big performer in the big games, Otis gave an MVP performance in the 1980 World Series, leading the team with a .478 average. He hit .279 in the four championship series against the Yankees.

Amos' play electrified and thrilled Royals fans, and he was a big part of the team's stretch of division winners.

1. What team did Otis start his Major League career with?

2. How did the Royals acquire him?

3. What year did Amos lead the American League in stolen bases?

4. Which one of Otis' teammates finished second in stolen bases that year?

5. What year did Otis start in the All-Star game?

6. How many All-Star games was he selected for?

7. On September 7, 1971, Otis accomplished something that hadn't happened in the American League in 44 years. What did he do and against what team?

8. When did he win his first Gold Glove?

9. How many Gold Gloves did Otis win?

10. What team did Otis finish his career with?

Dan Quisenberry

I broke my slump when I found a delivery in my flaw.

Dan Quisenberry

You can't be thinking about too many things. Relief pitchers have to get into a zone of their own. I just hope I'm stupid enough.

Dan Quisenberry

Forget about the funny things he said through the course of his career and the side-winding, submarine, slingshot fling of a pitch he threw. The Quiz was outstanding, one of the best relief aces the game has ever seen. In a six-year period (1980-85), no one in the AL was better.

Dan used his slider and an incredible penchant for control to befuddle American League hitters during his career. A workhorse for the Royals pitching staff, Dan threw more than 125 innings for the club five different times. His presence in the bullpen is what finally pushed the team over the top and into the World Series in 1980. And when the pitching staff fell on hard times in 1983, he held it together, garnering a Major League record number of saves.

Despite his pitching talents, Dan might best be remembered for his wit, quotes, outlook on life and love of the game of baseball. He was always fast to remind fans that he knew how lucky he was to be a baseball player. Royals' fans knew they were lucky he played in Kansas City, and with his tragic passing at the end of the 1998 season, the Royals, Kansas City and all of baseball lost one of the truly great men to grace the playing fields of the Major Leagues.

1. When did Quiz appear in his first Royals game?

2. When did he earn his first save?

3. How many times did Quiz lead the AL in saves?

4. What is the name of the award given to the top relief pitcher in each league?

5. By the end of the 1984 season, Dan accomplished something that had never been done in the majors before. What did he do?

6. How many different colleges did Quiz attend, and what are their names?

7. How many All-Star games was Quiz selected for?

8. Did Dan ever start a game in the Majors?

9. Quiz pitched for two other teams at the end of his career. Who were they?

10. How many games did Quiz appear in for the Royals?

Dan Quisenberry

11. How many times did he lead the American League in games pitched?

I had wild dreams (about playing Major League Baseball), but when I got old enough to realize how hard it is to get signed and how tough it is, I never thought I'd make it. I was surprised that I did. Sometimes in the off season I'll drive to the ballpark and I'll look at the ballpark and think 'that's my place of employment' and then it really hits me, what I do.

Dan Quisenberry, 1985

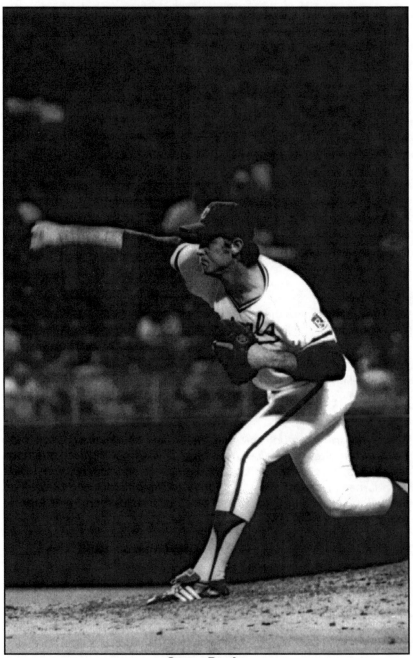

Steve Busby

Steve Busby

Steve Busby ripped through the American League his first two seasons with the Royals. He won 40 games, tossed two no-hitters, and as if there was any doubt to his pitching ability, set an American League record by putting down 33 consecutive batters in one stretch. No question, he was the Royals first great pitcher. And it is no stretch to say Cooperstown was in his future.

A rotator cuff injury basically ended his career—1975 was the last time he started more than 30 games—and while he dabbled with the club on and off through 1980, Busby was pitching more from memory and guile than physical talent. He won three games in 1976, missed all of the 1977 season, and won another eight games before quitting for good after the 1980 season.

Steve left his mark on the club and Major League Baseball during his short stint, and established many team records with his competitive, tough spirit and pitching prowess. Imagine: what if the Royals had had a healthy Steve Busby throughout the late '70s and '80s?

1. What university did Steve attend?

2. When did Steve make his debut with the Royals?

3. How many All-Star games was Steve selected for?

4. How many times was Busby the Opening Day pitcher for the Royals?

5. What award did Steve win in 1973?

6. Steve did something special in just his 10th Major League start. What was it?

7. When and where did he throw his two no-hitters?

8. How many games did he win for the Royals in his career?

9. What other Major League teams did Steve pitch for?

10. What was Steve's career high for strikeouts in a game?

Dennis Leonard

Dennis pitched two no-hitters in the minors, tossed countless big-game wins for the Royals, and was considered the team's money pitcher for most of his career. He was also the Majors winningest righthanded pitcher from 1975-81, chalking up 130 victories in that time span. Yet he might best be remembered for his return to the Royals after nearly three years on the disabled list and four knee operations; Dennis pitched a dramatic 1-0 complete game win over the Blue Jays at Royals Stadium on April 12, 1986. That one game, maybe more than any other in his terrific career, showed his determination, will and ability, and why he was a great pitcher.

Dennis won the Royals Pitcher of the Year Award three times, and holds the club record for complete games, strikeouts and shutouts. He faced his hardest luck in the ALCS, losing three times to the Yankees. But he also won the important second game of the 1980 ALCS, a win that was a big step in the Royals sweep of the New Yorkers that year.

1. How did the Royals acquire Dennis?

2. Where did Dennis go to high school?

3. In college, Dennis was an all-conference selection. Where did he attend college?

4. When did Dennis make his Major League debut?

5. Dennis Leonard won 144 games for the Royals in 12 seasons. How many times did he win 20 or more games?

6. How many games did he lose in his career?

7. In 1979 Dennis led the AL in one pitching category. What was it?

8. Dennis tied for the American League lead in wins once. What year did he accomplish this?

9. Dennis led the American League in one other pitching category in 1981. What was the category, and the number posted by Dennis?

10. Dennis led the American League in games started three times. What three years did he lead?

Dennis Leonard

Cookie Rojas

Born in Havana, Cuba, on March 6, 1939, Cookie was one of the first stars to play in Kansas City, bringing several skills to the field of play when he joined the Royals in 1970. He teamed with Fred Patek to give KC a talented keystone combo, and was instrumental in the team's rise to the top of the AL West. Voted the American League's top second baseman in 1971, Cookie led the junior circuit in fielding percentage that season with a .991 mark.

An all-time favorite of the Kansas City fans, Cookie made a comfortable shift into a utility role after Frank White took over second base, and still made winning contributions to the team through the 1977 season. He finished his career with 1,660 hits, a .263 batting average, and led the American League in fielding percentage twice.

1. What team did Cookie begin his career with?

2. What pitcher did Cookie collect his first Major League hit off of?

3. How many times was Cookie selected for the All-Star team as a Royal?

4. He was selected once for the National League. What team was he playing for, and in what year did he represent them?

5. How many hits did Rojas have in All-Star competition?

6. How many times in his career did Cookie hit .300 or better?

7. How did the Royals acquire Cookie?

8. Who was the second baseman Cookie replaced in the lineup?

9. In 1988, Cookie took on the managerial duties of what team?

Cookie Rojas

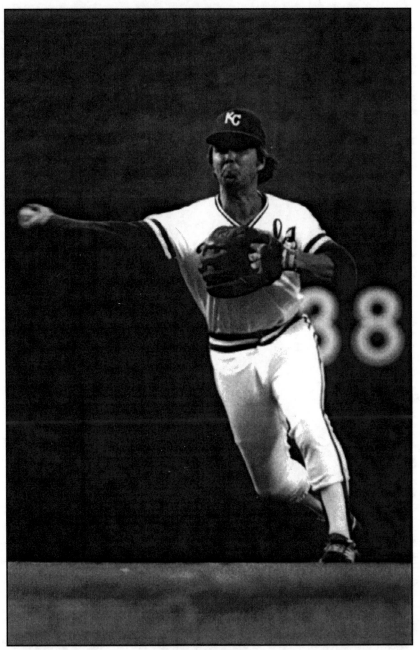

Fred Patek

Fred Patek

How short it too short? Fred Patek held the distinction of being the shortest player in the Major Leagues throughout his career. He proved, however, that good things come in small packages. After joining Kansas City in 1971, the slick-fielding shortstop quickly established himself as a catalyst at the plate and in the field. Patek's prowess for stealing bases helped the Royals score runs. In the field, he led AL shortstops in double plays four consecutive seasons, 1971-74.

A hitter when it counted most, Patek batted .389 in both the 1976 and 1977 ALCS. He hit a home run in the Royals only win of the 1978 ALCS. With the exception of home runs and batting average, Patek remains in the top ten of almost all of the Royals career batting records. Patek was always a fan favorite, and played 1,245 games for the Royals.

1. The Royals acquired Freddie Patek in a six-player deal with what team?

2. What two players came to the Royals with Patek?

3. How tall is Freddie?

4. How many times did Patek lead the American League in stolen bases?

5. True or False: Patek led the league in triples three times.

6. How many All-Star games was Patek selected for?

7. What team did Patek finish his career with?

8. Patek hit for the cycle in 1971 off what Minnesota pitcher?

9. How many lifetime stolen bases does Patek have?

10. What was Patek's lifetime batting average?

Mark Gubicza

Of all the strong, young arms the Royals had on their staff in the early 1980s, it seemed that if any one of them was expendable, it would be Mark Gubicza. Yet one by one the Royals dismantled the staff; first Danny Jackson, then Charlie Leibrandt and Bret Saberhagen. Through it all Gubicza remained, not leaving until after the 1996 season.

Gubicza left his mark on the Royals record book. He is third on the all-time win list, second in career starts, innings pitched and career losses. Gubicza compiled steady, unspectacular numbers throughout his career in a Royals uniform, and maybe that was the secret that kept him in Kansas City. He never had a truly horrible season, except 1996, and always kept the team in the game.

His departure from Kansas City marked the end of an era; he was the last of the 1985 world champs that was still with the club.

1. Where did Mark go to high school?

2. When did Mark pitch in his first game for the Royals? Against what team?

3. When did Mark earn his first Major League victory?

4. How many career wins for the Royals does Mark have?

5. How many All-Star games was Gubicza selected for?

6. How many games of the 1985 World Series did Mark pitch in?

7. What season did Mark win 20 games?

8. Mark holds the club record for strikeouts in a game. How many, and against what team did he set the record?

9. In 1988 Mark finished third in the AL Cy Young Award voting. What two pitchers finished ahead of him?

Kevin Appier

Kevin Appier took his place among the other great Royals pitchers in 1997 by posting his 100th win for the club. The combative Lancaster, California, native has been the ace of the Royals staff since 1995, and one of the top pitchers in the American League since 1992. Appier's long-reaching, hard deliveries are a staple around the American League, and his slider is considered the best in the league for a righthander. While his win totals haven't always measured up among the top pitchers in the league, his other numbers have. He consistently posts a low ERA, his best coming in 1992 at 2.46. His fiery, competitive nature is always evident on the mound.

Appier finished the 1997 season as the sixth winningest pitcher in the club's history with 105 wins, and is fifth in career ERA (pitchers with 500 innings pitched). He is already fourth in career games started with 247, and 10th in complete games. If he can recover completely from his shoulder ailments and stays with the team, Kevin should make a run at a lot of other club records.

1. What two colleges did Appier attend?

2. How did the Royals acquire Kevin Appier?

3. When did he pitch in his first game for the Royals?

4. When did he win his first game for the Royals?

5. When did Appier win his 100th game?

6. How many times has Appier appeared in the All-Star game?

7. Kevin won the American League ERA title in 1993. What was his ERA that season?

8. How many times has Appier been the Opening Day pitcher for KC?

9. How many times in his career has Appier recorded 200 or more strikeouts in a season?

10. Kevin became the first Royal and 27th Major League pitcher to achieve this feat. What is it?

Jeff Montgomery

The Royals all-time leader in saves, Jeff fell into the closer role much as Dan Quisenberry had a decade earlier and quickly established himself as one of the best in the Majors. He became Kansas City's closer by the process of elimination, but he also came very close to never getting the opportunity to show the Royals what he could do.

On the verge of being sent to the minors during spring training in 1989, it was suggested to Jeff by one of his coaches that he simply throw the ball over the plate—and so he did. Since then his pitching has always been solid. His use of four different pitches in closing situations is a bit of a deviation from the normal closer, but it has proven to be his strongest point. After his initial success, Montgomery rewrote the Royals relief pitching statistics and records, appearing 637 games for Kansas City since 1988.

The 1997 season started with Jeff coming off shoulder surgery rehabilitation, and after he took the mound a few times, his effectiveness appeared to be gone. But he corrected his problems and after finishing strong in 1997, notched 36 saves in 1998 again to lead the club.

1. What university did Jeff attend?

2. When and how did the Royals acquire Jeff?

3. When did Jeff appear in his first game for the Royals?

4. How many career starts does Jeff have?

5. When did Montgomery record his first Major League save?

6. Jeff has won one Rolaids Relief Man award. What year did he win?

7. How many All-Star games has Jeff been selected for?

8. How many career saves does Jeff have?

9. How many career wins does Jeff have?

Jeff Montgomery

John Mayberry

John Mayberry

A Detroit native, Big John came to the Royals in one of the club's best trades and immediately became the big hitter on the team. He swatted 25 homers and knocked in 100 runs in his first season with Kansas City, and continued to produce top offensive numbers throughout his stay with the Royals. His best season was 1975, when he crashed 34 home runs, batted .291 and collected 106 RBIs. Always extremely agile around first base, John was considered one of the best fielding first basemen in the American League. Twice he led the league in fielding percentage.

Mayberry's numbers dropped dramatically in 1976 (.232 BA, 13 HR), and while he rebounded a bit and hit 23 home runs in 1977, his batting average was again low at .230. Royals manager Whitey Herzog demanded the club trade Mayberry following the 1977 ALCS, giving owner Ewing Kauffman an "either him or me" ultimatum. Big John was shipped to Toronto before the start of the 1978 season.

Despite his relatively short stay in Kansas City, Mayberry remains a fan favorite, and is still in the top 10 of many of the club's offensive records.

1. What team traded Mayberry to the Royals, and who else was in involved in the trade?

2. John led the American League in this category twice, in 1973 and again in 1975. What's the category, and how many?

3. How many times was Mayberry selected for the All-Star team?

4. How many home runs did Mayberry hit as a Royal?

5. How many home runs did Mayberry hit in the 1976 ALCS?

6. How many times in his career did John hit three home runs in a game?

7. Mayberry led the American League in on-base percentage once. What year did he do it, and what was the percentage?

8. John finished second in the American League MVP voting in 1975. Who won the award that season?

9. What was Mayberry's lifetime batting average?

10. What team did he finish his career with?

Paul Splittorff

The Royals all-time winningest pitcher, Splitt was the mainstay of the team's early pitching staffs, and an important member during the championship years in the late '70s. He logged more than 1,000 Ks in his career, and is Kansas City's all-time leader in games started with 392.

A clutch performer, Splitt always pitched well for the team in the playoffs, and it is still a puzzle to many fans why he didn't pitch more in the 1980 World Series. He now enjoys a view of the game from the broadcast booth at Kauffman Stadium, and has enlightened viewers and listeners with his baseball expertise for more than 10 seasons.

1. What college did Splitt attend?

2. When did Paul make his first appearance for the Royals?

3. When did Paul pick up his first win for the Royals?

4. Paul was the first Royal to win 20 games in a season. What season did he accomplish this?

5. Paul has won more games than any other pitcher in Royals history. How many wins does he have?

6. Paul also has the distinction of losing more games than any other Royals pitcher. How many times did he lose in his career?

7. How many career strikeouts does Paul have?

8. Paul appeared in four different ALCS. What is his overall won-lost record for the ALCS?

9. Splitt never threw a no-hitter, but came close several times. How many one-hitters did he pitch?

10. Since his retirement, Paul has done color commentary for both the Royals radio and TV networks. True or false?

ROYAL
NUMBERS

Career Leaders

Battting

Games
2,707 George Brett
2,324 Frank White
1,891 Amos Otis
1,837 Hal McRae
1,787 Willie Wilson
1,245 Fred Patek

At-bats
10,349 George Brett
7,859 Frank White
7,050 Amos Otis
6,799 Willie Wilson
6,568 Hal McRae

Runs
1,583 George Brett
1,074 Amos Otis
1,060 Willie Wilson
912 Frank White
873 Hal McRae

Hits
3,154 George Brett
2,006 Frank White
1,977 Amos Otis
1,968 Willie Wilson
1,924 Hal McRae

Doubles
665 George Brett
449 Hal McRae
407 Frank White
365 Amos Otis
241 Willie Wilson

Triples
137 George Brett
133 Willie Wilson
65 Amos Otis
63 Hal McRae

Home Runs
317 George Brett
193 Amos Otis
169 Hal McRae
160 Frank White
143 John Mayberry

Runs Batted In
1,595 George Brett
1,012 Hal McRae
992 Amos Otis
886 Frank White
552 John Mayberry

Batting Average
(minimum 500 games)
.305 George Brett
.294 Kevin Seitzer
.293 Wally Joyner
.293 Hal McRae
.290 Danny Tartabull

Stolen Bases
612 Willie Wilson
340 Amos Otis
336 Fred Patek
201 George Brett
178 Frank White

Pitching

Earned-run Average
(minimum 500 innings)
2.55 Dan Quisenberry
2.97 Jeff Montgomery
3.05 Steve Farr
3.21 Bret Saberhagen
3.30 Kevin Appier

Wins
166 Paul Splittorff
144 Dennis Leonard
132 Mark Bubicza
111 Larry Gura
110 Bret Saberhagen
105 Kevin Appier

Losses
143 Paul Splittorff
135 Mark Gubicza
106 Dennis Leonard
80 Kevin Appier
78 Larry Gura

Innings Pitched
2,554.2 Paul Splittorff
2,218.2 Mark Gubicza
2,187.0 Dennis Leonard
1,701.1 Larry Gura
1,680.1 Kevin Appier

Strikeouts
1,373 Kevin Appier
1,366 Mark Gubicza
1,323 Dennis Leonard
1,093 Bret Saberhagen
1,057 Paul Splittorff

Bases on Balls
783 Mark Gubicza
780 Paul Splittorff
622 Dennis Leonard
587 Tom Gordon
573 Kevin Appier

Games
637 Jeff Montgomery
573 Dan Quisenberry
429 Paul Splittorff
382 Mark Gubicza
312 Dennis Leonard

Shutouts
23 Dennis Leonard
17 Paul Splittorff
16 Mark Gubicza
14 Larry Gura
14 Bret Saberhagen

Saves
292 Jeff Montgomery
238 Dan Quisenberry
58 Doug Bird
49 Steve Farr
40 Ted Abernathy
31 Al Hrabosky

Single Season Records

Battting

At-bats	.705	Willie Wilson	1980
Runs	.133	Willie Wilson	1980
Hits	.230	Willie Wilson	1980
Singles	.184	Willie Wilson	1980
Doubles	.54	Hal McRae	1977
Triples	.21	Willie Wilson	1985
Home Runs	.36	Steve Balboni	1985
Grand Slams	.3	Danny Tartabull	1988
RBIs	.133	Hal McRae	1982
Walks	.122	John Mayberry	1973
Batting Average	.390	George Brett	1980
Slugging Pct.	.664	George Brett	1980
Stolen Bases	.83	Willie Wilson	1979

Pitching

Games	.84	Dan Quisenberry	1985
Complete Games	.21	Dennis Leonard	1977
Innings	.294.2	Dennis Leonard	1978
Wins	.23	Bret Saberhagen	1989
Losses	.19	Paul Splittorff	1974
Winning pct.	.793	Bret Saberhagen	1989
Walks	.120	Mark Gubicza	1987
Strikouts	.244	Dennis Leonard	1977
Shutouts	.6	Roger Nelson	1972
Home runs allowed	.33	Dennis Leonard	1979
Lowest ERA	.2.08	Roger Nelson	1972
Saves	.45	Dan Quisenberry	1983
		Jeff Montgomery	1993

Year-by-Year Results

Year	Position	Won	Lost	Pct.	GB
1969	Fourth	69	93	.426	28
1970	Fourth(Tied)	65	97	.401	33
1971	Second	85	76	.528	16
1972	Fourth	76	78	.494	16.5
1973	Second	88	74	.543	6
1974	Fifth	77	85	.475	13
1975	Second	91	71	.562	7
1976	First	90	72	.556	+2.5
1977	First	102	60	.630	+8
1978	First	92	70	.567	+5
1979	Second	85	77	.525	3
1980	First	97	65	.599	+14
1981	Fourth	50	53	.485	11
1982	Second	90	72	.556	3
1983	Second	79	83	.488	20
1984	First	84	78	.519	+3
1985	First	91	71	.562	+1
1986	Third (Tied)	76	86	.469	16
1987	Second	83	79	.512	2
1988	Third	84	77	.522	19.5
1989	Second	92	70	.568	7
1990	Sixth	75	86	.466	27.5
1991	Sixth	82	80	.506	13
1992	Fifth (Tied)	72	90	.444	24
1993	Third	84	78	.519	10
1994	Third	64	51	.557	4
1995	Second	70	74	.486	30
1996	Fifth	75	86	.466	24
1997	Fifth	67	93	.419	19
1998	Third	72	89	.447	16.5

MORE
TRIVIA

Ewing Kauffman

Ewing Kauffman

When Kansas City needed someone to step up and take control of the city's baseball fortunes, Ewing Kauffman took over and hit a grand slam. Through his guidance, leadership, integrity and strong ownership, the Royals achieved overwhelming success. Mr. K wanted to give Kansas City a winning baseball team, and he delivered. The Royals became one of the top franchises in the Major Leagues, winning six division titles, two American League pennants and a World Series championship during his tenure as the club's top man.

1. When did Ewing Kauffman purchase the team that was to become the Royals?

2. Where was Mr. Kauffman born?

3. What branch of the Armed Services did Mr. K serve in?

4. What year did Mr. K start the pharmaceutical firm that later became Marion Labs?

5. In what year did the Kansas City Press Club vote Mr. K their Man-of-the-Year?

6. What date was the Royals Stadium name changed to Kauffman Stadium?

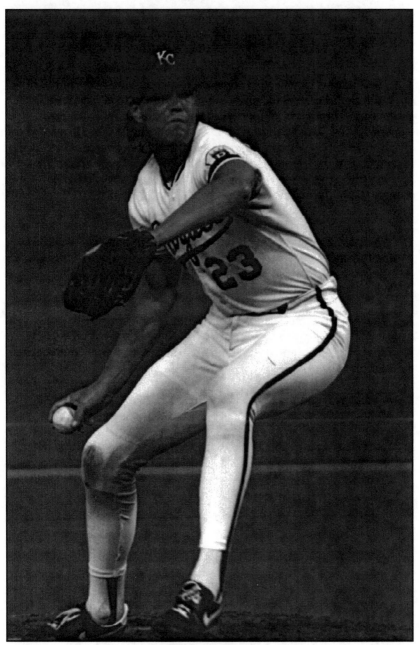

Mark Gubicza

Pitchers

1. This pitcher set the club record for the most wins by a rookie pitcher. Who is he?

2. Who is the only three-time 20-game winner in Royals history?

3. When this pitcher made his first start for the Royals, he was the youngest pitcher ever to start a game for the Royals. Who is he, and how old was he?

4. Only one pitcher in Royals history has ever struck out four batters in an inning. Who is the pitcher?

5. The highest win total in a season by a Royals pitcher is 23. Who holds this record?

6. This pitcher holds the club record for the most consecutive wins during a season. Who is he, how many did he win in a row, and what year did he accomplish the mark?

7. Who was the Royals first 20-game winner, and what season did he post the 20 wins?

8. This pitcher twice posted the lowest ERA on the Royals, first in 1974, and again in 1976. Who is he?

9. The club record for complete games is 21, set in 1977. Who set the mark?

10. This pitcher held the Royals record for saves in a season, 23, until Quisenberry broke it in 1980 with 33. Who had this record?

11. The most starts ever by a KC pitcher was done in 1978. Who did it, and how many?

12. Only three pitchers in club history have ever posted 200-strikeout seasons. Who are they, and when did they top the 200 K mark?

13. Has any Royals pitcher ever pitched 300 innings in a single season?

14. Who holds the club record for the lowest ERA in a season (starters)?

15. Who holds the Royals record for the most losses in a season?

16. This pitcher tossed 6 shutouts for Kansas City in 1972, still the top mark in club history. Who is he?

17. Three pitchers have lost more than 100 games in Royals history. Who are they, and how many games did each lose?

18. This pitcher has been the Royals Opening Day starter more than anyone else, taking the mound 6 times to start the season. Who is he?

19. Only one pitcher has ever won a Gold Glove Award for the Royals. Who is he, and what year did he win the award?

20. Who was the Royals first (1969) Opening Day pitcher?

21. Two different pitchers have won the Cy Young Award while playing for the Royals. Who are they, and when did they win the award?

22. This pitcher won the Cy Young Award in the National League and signed as a free agent with the Royals the following season. Who is he?

23. This Hall-of-Famer won more than 300 games and finished his career with Kansas City. Who is he and what year did he pitch for the Royals?

24. This pitcher led the Royals in saves in 1978 and 1979. Who is he?

Catchers

1. Darrell Porter joined the Royals in December 1976, but was not the Opening Day catcher at the start of the 1977 season. Who was?

2. Jim Sundberg spent the majority of his career with the Texas Rangers, but what team did he come to the Royals from?

3. Only one catcher has won a Gold Glove Award while playing with the Royals. Who is that catcher, and what year did he win the award?

4. Who was the Royals Opening Day catcher in 1980?

5. Who was the Royals Opening Day catcher in 1969?

6. Who holds the Royals season record for the most RBIs by a catcher?

7. Mike MacFarlane left Kansas City for one season, 1995, and returned for the 1996 season. What team did he play with in 1995?

8. This catcher was the Royals top draft pick in 1989. He played with Kansas City from 1990 through 1995, and then went to the Mets. Who is he?

9. This catcher had his best seasons with the Royals, but won the World Series MVP with a National League team. Who is he?

Jamie Quirk

10. Who was the Royals Opening Day catcher in 1987?

11. The Royals opening day catcher from 1974-76, this backstop was traded to the Yankees for Larry Gura on May 16, 1976. Who is he?

Darrell Porter

First Basemen

1. Who was the Royals Opening Day first baseman in 1969?

2. His first team was the Yankees, and he returned there after leaving KC. He also played for Seattle and Texas. Who is he?

3. Willie Aikens came to Kansas City in 1980 from what American League team?

4. This Royal started at first in 1971 after opening in the outfield in 1969 and at third base in 1970. Who is he?

5. This Royal played 92 consecutive games at first base between 1976 and 1979 without committing an error. Who is he?

6. A highly publicized rookie, this Royal took over first base at the start of the 1978 season. Who is he?

7. Wally Joyner came to Kansas City from California as a free agent before the 1992 season. What team was he traded to after the 1995 season?

8. Steve Balboni was the main first baseman from 1984-86, and also a little in 1987. Who was the first baseman in 1983?

9. John Mayberry debuted for the Royals in 1972. What team did Kansas City acquire him from?

10. Who started at first base in 1996's Opening Day game?

11. This player filled in at first and played an important backup role for the Royals from 1977 through 1980. He came to Kansas City from the Chicago Cubs. Who is he?
12. He was the Opening Day starter at first base in 1987, but started at third from 1988 through 1991. Who is he?

13. John Mayberry was traded before the season started in 1978. What team did the Royals send him to?

14. Only two Royals first basemen have been selected for the All-Star game. Who are they?

Second Basemen

1. Who was the Royals Opening Day second baseman in 1969?

2. Luis Alcaraz started the 1970 season at second. Who took his place in June?

3. How many consecutive seasons was Frank White the Opening Day second baseman?

4. Who replaced Frank in the starting lineup at the beginning of the 1991 season?

5. He was one of the Royals top utility players in 1976, appearing in 46 games at second base and 22 at DH. He also stole 15 bases that season. Who is he?

6. He played 61 games at second base in 1994, 84 games in 1996. He was traded just before the start of the 1997 season to Atlanta. Who is he? .

7. Bobby Knoop filled in at second base for Kansas City, appearing in 52 games in 1971 and 33 in 1972. What two teams did he play for before coming to K.C.?

8. This versatile utility player was the Royals second baseman in 93 games during the 1992 season, but played there only three more times through the 1995 season. Who is he?

9. A fixture in the Royals infield in the late '70s and early '80s, this player was the club's main shortstop for five years. But he also appeared in more than 100 game at second base during his career. Who is he?

Third Basemen

1. Who was the Royals starting third baseman in 1969?

2. Who played third most of the time in 1970?

3. Who was the Royals Opening Day starting third baseman from 1971 through 1974?

4. When did George Brett become the regular third baseman?

5. After starting at first base, this rookie took over third, with Brett moving to first. Who is he?

6. While Brett was on the DL during the 1984 season, this utility man played a key role in the Royals drive to the AL West title with his fielding and hitting. Who is he?

7. After productive seasons in Minnesota and California, this third sacker's best years appeared to be behind him when he signed with KC in 1993. Who is he?

8. Who holds the Royals record for the most home runs hit by a third baseman?

9. What team did the Royals acquire Dean Palmer from?

10. How many Gold Glove awards have Kansas City third basemen won?

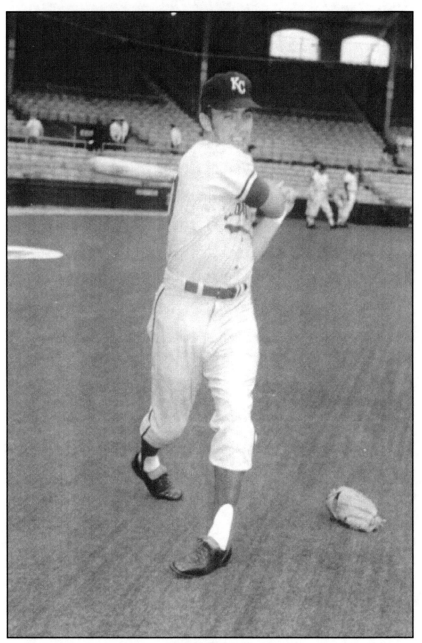

Paul Schaal

Shortstops

1. Who was the Royals Opening Day shortstop in 1969?

2. How many times was Fred Patek the Royals starting shortstop on Opening Day?

3. Who replaced Fred Patek as the Royals shortstop in the starting lineup?

4. The Royals primarily used two shortstops in 1985. Who are they?

5. Who was the Opening Day shortstop in 1986?

6. Who did the Royals trade to acquire Kurt Stillwell?

7. This shortstop was with the Royals from 1970 through 1974 and was in the starting lineup on Opening Day in 1972. Who is he?

8. The Royals signed this shortstop away from division rival Minnesota, and he was their starting shortstop from 1993 through 1995. Who is he?

9. This player, while primarily a shortstop, has also played second and third base, as well as the outfield, for Kansas City. But in 1992, he was the Opening Day shortstop. Who is he?

10. What teams did U.L. Washington play for after he left the Royals?

11. This infielder played 29 games at shortstop for the Royals in 1974, 42 in 1975, and 37 in 1976. Who is he?

12. Who was the backup shortstop when the Royals won the American League in 1980?

13. The Royals used three different shortstops in 1970. Who were they?

14. This infielder played at least one game at shortstop every year from 1974 through 1978. Who is he?

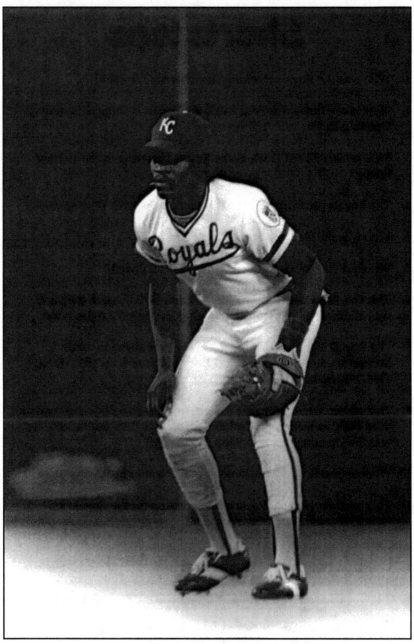

U. L. Washington

Outfielders

1. What three players made up the Royals opening day outfield in 1969?

2. Lou Piniella won the 1969 American League Rookie of the Year award. What team did the Royals acquire him from?

3. After a long, productive career with the Reds, this outfielder played for St. Louis, Cleveland and California before finishing up in Kansas City in 1974-75. Who is he?

4. After Piniella was traded, who initially took his spot in the outfield?

5. This outfielder finished second in the American League MVP voting for the 1977 season, then never received another MVP vote the rest of his career. Who is he?

6. This outfielder hit .302 and .292 in '76 and '77, then played for Boston and Texas before returning to the Royals in 1982 to end his career. Who is he?

7. How many different outfielders have won a Gold Glove while playing for Kansas City?

8. This outfielder was in the Royals starting lineup on opening day, 1977, but was out of baseball after the 1979 season. Who is he?
   Joe Zdeb

9. He played several positions, but was primarily an outfielder who was in the Royals starting lineup at the beginning of the 1978, 1979, 1980 and 1981 season. He finished his career playing with the Reds, Mets and Cardinals. Who is he?

Pat Sheridan

Jim Eisenreich

10. The Royals traded John Morris to the Cardinals for this left fielder in 1985. Who is he?

11. Who did the Royals trade to Seattle to acquire Danny Tartabull?

12. Kansas City traded Rich Gale and Bill Laskey to the Giants for this outfielder, who played with the Royals in 1982-83. Who is he?

13. Hal McRae is one of two Royals to have played in 162 games in one season, and he did so in 1977. This outfielder is the other Royal to play in 162 games, and he also did it in 1977. Who is he?

14. George Brett led the AL in slugging average three times. This outfielder is the only other Royal to lead the league, and he did it in 1991. Who is he?

15. A prolific base-stealer in the National League, this outfielder played two seasons in Kansas City, accumulating 50 stolen bases in his one full season before being traded. Who is he?

16. This outfielder hit two home runs in the 1985 ALCS. He played for the Tigers, Giants and Yankees after leaving the Royals. Who is he?

17. When did Johnny Damon make his Major League debut?

Designated Hitters

1. Who was the Royals first designated hitter?

2. How many different DH's did Kansas City use in 1973, the first year of the rule?

3. Who was the Royals DH on opening day, 1975?

4. Who was the DH on Opening Day, 1976?

5. Who was the DH on Opening Day, 1985?

6. What position did Hal McRae play before settling into the DH spot in the lineup?

7. How many times was Hal McRae selected the American League Designated Hitter of the Year?

8. Before finishing his career as a DH, what position did George Brett play?

9. This former National League MVP was the Royals designated hitter for 26 games in 1974. Who is he?

10. This future Royal was the Phillies primary DH in the 1980 World Series. Who is he?

Ed Kirkpatrick

Managers

1. Through the 1998 season, how many managers have the Royals had?

2. Who was the Royals first manager?

3. This manager was a long-time coach under Earl Weaver of the Orioles before taking control of the Royals. Who is he?

4. Bob Lemon took over when this manager was fired 42 games into the 1970 season. Who is he?

5. How many former Royals players have managed the team, and who are they?

6. Which manager led the Royals to a first-place finish the second half of the 1981 season?

7. Which manager has served the longest?
8. Which manager has served the shortest amount of time?

9. Which Royals manager has the highest winning percentage (not counting interim managers)?

10. Who lost the most games?

11. Three different managers led the Royals to American League West Division Championships. Who are they?

12. How many games did the Royals win after Tony Muser became manager in 1997?

American League Championship Series

1976 ALCS
New York 3 games, Kansas City 2 games

We've got the kind of club that's going to be good for a long time to come. We're going to get better, but I don't think the Yankees are going to get better.

Hal McRae
after the Royals lost the 1976 ALCS

The Royals went into the 1976 ALCS just happy to be playing for the pennant. This series will always be remembered for Chris Chambliss hitting the pennant-winning home run for New York, but the Royals also provided several exciting moments as well, particularly George Brett's game-tying homer the inning before Chambliss' shot.

John Mayberry tries to pick off the Yankees Mickey Rivers during the '76 ALCS.

The closeness of this series was a foreshadowing of things to come as these two rivals would become well acquainted in the playoffs throughout the rest of the decade.

1. Two Royals hit home runs in this series. Who hit the homers, and in what games did they homer in?

2. Who started Game 1 for the Royals?

3. This pitcher started two games in the series, but didn't figure in either decision. Who is he?

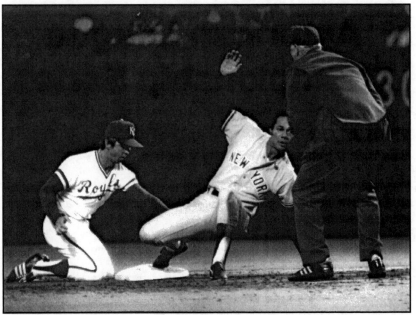

Fred Patek puts a tag on the Yankees Roy White in 1976 ALCS action.

4. This pitcher relieved Larry Gura in Game 4 and got the win. Who is he?

5. Who had the highest batting average for the Royals in the series?

6. Amos Otis was hurt running to the bag in his first at bat of Game 1 and missed the rest of the series. Who replaced him in the outfield?

7. Who was on base when Brett hit his game-tying, three-run homer in Game 5?

8. Which Kansas City pitcher gave up the series-ending home run to the Yankees Chris Chambliss?

9. How many bases did the Royals steal in the series?

1977 ALCS
New York 3 games, Kansas City 2 games

It looks like we can't get a World Series in this town.
Whitey Herzog, after 1977 ALCS

The heartbreak of 1976 was nothing compared to the devastating loss the Royals suffered in the 1977 ALCS. Up two games to one, Kansas City dropped the last two games at Royals Stadium, losing Game 5 in the 9th inning. The Yankees waltzed on to the World Series; the Royals added perhaps the hardest loss in the team's short history to their legacy.

1. Who started and won Game 1 of the 1977 ALCS for the Royals?

2. Three Royals homered in Game 1. Who were they?

3. How many home runs did the Royals hit the rest of the series?

Fred Patek writhes in pain after being spiked by Reggie Jackson in Game 5 of the 1977 ALCS. Jackson, Frank White and George Brett look on. Patek continued to play in the game.

4. Who started Game 2 for the Royals?

5. Who started and pitched a complete game to win Game 3?

6. Who had three hits, including a double and triple, scored two runs and had an RBI in Game 4 for the Royals in a losing effort?

7. Who was the losing pitcher for the Royals in Game 5?

8. Who hit .444, the team high for KC in the series?

9. Who had an RBI pinch-hit single for the Yankees in the eighth inning to make the score 3-2 Royals?

10. Who made the last out for the Royals in Game 5, ending the series?

1978 ALCS
New York 3 games, Kansas City 1 game

Man, I want to beat these guys soooo bad!
Frank White, before the '78 series

L osing for the third year in a row was no easier than the first two times, but it didn't take as long. Kansas City might have played the Yankees tougher than in the two previous series, but could only win one time against the Bronx Bombers. George Brett hit three home runs in Game 3, and still the Yankees found a way to win. And as they did the year before, the Yankees went on to win the World Series.

1. The Yankees had to win a one-game divisional playoff to qualify for the ALCS. Who did they beat to win the Eastern division?

2. The Royals won Game 2 of the series, 10-4. Who was the winning pitcher for Kansas City?

3. George Brett hit three home runs in Game 3 off the same pitcher. Who was the Yankee pitcher?

4. Who hit the game-winning home run for the Yankees in Game 3?

5. Who was the only other Royal to hit a home run in the series?

6. Which pitcher lost two of the three games for the Royals?

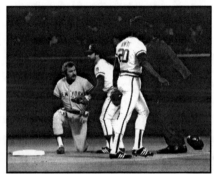

New York's Thurman Munson prepares to leave the field after being thrown out in Game 2 action. Patek made the play as White looks on.

Pete LaCock hits in Game 2.

1980 ALCS
Kansas City 3 games, New York 0 games

Our fans think we've already won the World Series by beating the Yankees.

George Brett
after the Royals won the 1980 ALCS

Finally! After three futile tries against the Yankees, the Royals finally hit the jackpot and won the American League Championship Series. The Yankees did not go quietly though, as it took a dramatic three-run home run by George Brett in Game 3 to bring the AL pennant home to KC for the first time ever. Frank White also starred for the guys in blue, capturing the series MVP award.

1. Who started and won Game 1 of the series for Kansas City?

2. Who homered for Kansas City in Game 1?

3. Who pitched eight plus innings in Game 2, struck out eight batters and got the win for the Royals?

George Brett receives congratulations from Lance Mulliniks after homering in Game 1 of the 1980 ALCS.

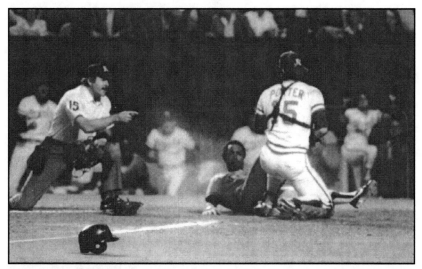

In one of the key plays of the '80 ALCS, Royals catcher Darrell Porter looks back as Home Plate Umpire Ed Brinkman's calls the Yankee runner out. George Brett made the peg that cut down what would have been the tying run.

4. George Brett made a perfect peg to the plate to cut down the potential tying run in the top of the eighth inning of Game 2. Who was the Yankee runner he gunned down?

5. Frank White was the 1980 ALCS MVP. How many home runs did he hit in the series?

Dennis Leonard, Jim Frey George Brett and Darrell Porter try to sort things out during Game 2.

6. Who was the winning pitcher for the Royals in Game 3?

7. How many saves did Quiz have in the series?

8. Who was on base when Brett hit his pennant-winning home run in the seventh inning of Game 3?

1981 Divisional Playoff
Oakland 3 games, Kansas City 0 games

With the players strike wiping out two months of the season, the Royals were able to rebound from their poor start and, after a change in managers, capture the second half division title. The Oakland A's quickly proved who the division champs were, though, and took out Kansas City in three games.

1. Why was there a divisional play-off in 1981?

2. How many home runs did the Royals hit in the series?

3. How many runs did the Royals score in the series?

4. The Royals lost Game 2, 2-1. Who was the losing pitcher for KC?

5. Who was the losing pitcher for Kansas City in Game 3?

John Wathan argues a point in the '81 Divisional playoff.

1984 ALCS
Detroit 3 games, Kansas City 0 games

Kansas City returned to the ALCS after a three-year absence, but were a little overmatched by the eventual world champion Detroit Tigers. The Royals played the Tigers tough in Games 2 and 3, but ran out of gas. The team provided a nice sneak peak to next season's club.

1. Who was the Royals starter in Game 1?

2. Who started Game 2 for KC?

3. Who hit a home run for the Tigers in the Game 2?

4. The Royals lost Game 2 in extra innings. Who was the losing pitcher?

5. Who pitched a complete-game 3-hitter against the Tigers in Game 3, but lost, 1-0?

6. Who was the Royals leading hitter in the series?

Detroit's Sparky Anderson and KC's Dick Howser meet before the '84 ALCS.

1985 ALCS
Kansas City 4 games, Toronto 3 games

The difference between us and everyone else is George Brett.

Dane Iorg, Royals Utility Player

Kansas City pulled off one of the great comebacks in the history of the ALCS, overcoming a three games to one deficit, to beat the Blue Jays for the AL pennant. George Brett led the way with great hitting as the Royals returned to the World Series.

1. He had only four hits in the series for the Royals, but they were a single, double, triple and home run. He also had six RBIs. Who is he?

2. Charlie Leibrandt lost two of the games in the series for the Royals. Who lost the other game?

3. How many saves did Quiz have in the series?

4. Danny Jackson had a complete-game shutout and beat the Blue Jays, 2-0. What other game did he pitch in?

5. How many bases did the Royals steal in the series?

6. Who started Games 3 and 7 for KC, but didn't figure in either decision?

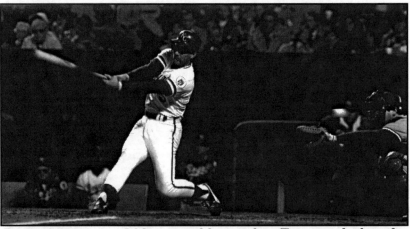

Brett slams one of his many hits against Toronto during the 1985 ALCS.

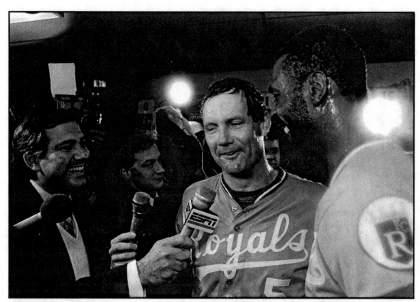

George Brett and Willie Wilson talk with reporters during the club's post-game celebration. Both players were key figures in the Royals series win.

7. Who was the winning pitcher in Game 7 for the Royals?

8. Who hit homers in Games 2 and 7 while playing right field for Kansas City?

9. This Toronto pitcher had two of the Blue Jays' three wins, getting both in relief. Who is he?

10. As a team, how many home runs did the Royals hit? And Toronto?

Hal McRae is safe at second in the 1985 ALCS.

11. How many homers did Brett hit?

12. Who was the series MVP?

George Brett and Bret Saberhagen take a break during Game 7 of the 1985 World Series.

The World Series

1980 World Series
Philadelphia 4 games, Kansas City 2 games

I'd be talking to other outfielders between innings and we'd say 'Damn, we just can't hold a lead.'
Willie Wilson
during the 1980 World Series

I thought our players were a little tight there...I thought the World Series atmosphere intimidated them a little bit.
Jim Frey
on the Royals playing in Philly

I'm frustrated, but there's nothing I can do about it. The more you move, the more it hurts.
George Brett
on his hemorrhoids during Game 2

It'll be nice to go home and see somebody friendly, somebody who uses nice four-letter words.
Dan Quisenberry
on the Philadelphia fans

After three near-misses, the Royals finally beat the Yankees and brought the World Series to Kansas City. It proved to be anti-climatic though, as the Royals seemed satisfied with their ALCS win and were happy just to be playing in the Series.

Amos Otis and Willie Aikens starred, and despite one of the most famous cases of hemorrhoids ever, George Brett also supplied some offense. But the pitching was shaky throughout the series, and Philadelphia made the most of the breaks presented to them and captured the championship.

Larry Gura in Game 5 of the 1980 World Series.

1. Who was the Royals Game 1 starter in Philadelphia?

2. Which Royals player hit a home run in his first World Series at-bat?

3. Which pitcher lost two games to the Phillies in the series?

4. Which Royal had 11 hits and led the team with a .478 batting average for the series?

5. How many home runs did the Royals hit in the series? How many did the Phillies hit?

6. How many stolen bases did the Royals have in the series?

Willie Aikens supplied a lot of power for the Royals in the '80 World Series.

7. Which Royal was thrown out at home twice, once in Game 1, and again in Game 5?

8. Who homered twice in Game 1, and hit two more in Game 4 to set a World Series record for two multihomer games?

9. Which Royal struck out with the bases loaded in the bottom of the 9th inning to end Game 5?

10. Who was on base for KC during that final strikeout in Game 5?

11. Who was the winning pitcher for the Royals in Game 4?

12. Which Philadelphia starter beat the Royals twice in the series?

13. How many home runs did Brett hit in the series?

14. Which three Royals hit .400 or better for the series?

15. Who had the most RBIs for Kansas City in the series?

16. The Phillies had only three home runs as a team. Who hit them?

Frank White and Clint Hurdle celebrate during Game 5 action.

17. How many RBIs did Hal McRae have for the series?

18. Who made the last out of the series?

Despite his problems, Brett still hit well in the series.

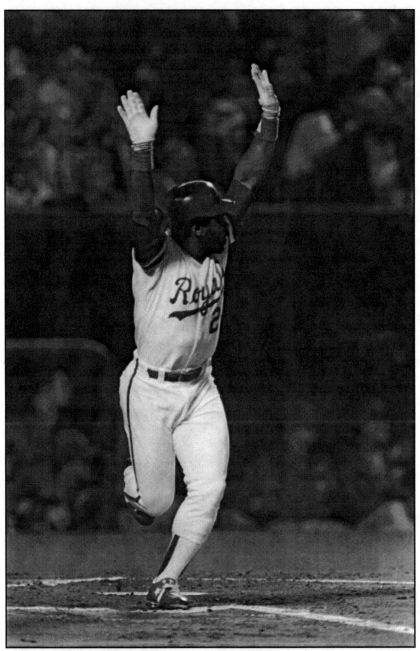

Darryl Motley celebrates as he watches his home run in Game 7 of the 1985 World Series leave the stadium.

1985 World Series
Kansas City 4 games, St. Louis 3 games

Any time you're down 2-0 in a short series, it's never easy. It's tough, but it's been done before. (Not after losing the first two games at home)

Dick Howser
after Game 2, won by St. Louis

We do have our backs to the wall. We have become friends with our backs to the wall. We know all the crevices.

Dan Quisenberry
after the Royals lost Game 4

Being down and out as much as we were and accomplishing what we did is unbelievable. These are special people. I've been on some great ballclubs in the '70s. This year we were a great ballclub, but this was a little different. This was a great ballclub inside.

George Brett
after winning the 1985 World Series

The improbable finish to an incredible season for the Royals—a World Series Championship! Kansas City completed the greatest season of comebacks by winning the final three games of the 1985 ALCS and then matched that feat by doing it again in the World Series. In the end, Kansas City embarrassed St. Louis with a Game 7 laugher to bring home the championship banner.

After dropping the first two games at home (no team in the history of the series had ever won after losing the first two games at home), the Royals fought back and took two out of three in St. Louis. A controversial call and outstanding pitching put the finishing touches on the comeback at Royals Stadium. Bret Saberhagen was the series star, but George Brett, as always, provided a lot of the offensive punch.

1. Who was the Royals starter in Game 1?

2. Which Cardinal starter defeated the Royals in Game 1?

3. Who was the losing pitcher for Kansas City in Game 2?

4. With the bases loaded in the ninth inning, who got the game-winning hit for the Cardinals that won Game 2?

Bret Saberhagen receives congratulations from manager Dick Howser and his teammates after defeating the Cardinals in Game 3.

5. Who was the Royals cleanup hitter in Game 3?

6. Bret Saberhagen started and won Game 3 for the Royals in St. Louis. Who was the Cardinals starter?

7. How many former Cardinal players were on the Royals World Series roster?

8. How many home runs did the Royals hit in the series? How many did the Cardinals hit?

9. How many stolen bases did the Royals have? The Cardinals?

10. Who was the Royals top hitter in the series?

11. Who was the Cardinals top hitter in the series?

Game 6 hitting hero Dane Iorg.

Game 6—Safe at First!

Cardinal fans have been whining about this game for more than a decade now, claiming a bad call cost their team a world championship. Nothing could be further from the truth. Shoddy play and an overall lack of composure hurt the Cardinals during the crucial plays that followed the call at first base in the bottom of the 9th inning of Game 6. KC took advantage of the mishaps—as championship team usually do—and pulled out a thrilling victory to force a Game 7. How much do you know about what happened during the Royals game-winning rally?

1. What was the score of Game 6 going into the bottom of the 9th?

2. Who led off for the Royals?

3. Who was pitching for St. Louis?

4. Who fielded the ball and threw to first?

5. Who covered the bag?

6. Who was the first base umpire who made the "controversial" call?

7. Who was the second hitter in the inning, and what happened during his at bat?

8. Who made the only out of the inning for Kansas City?

9. Who was at bat when Cardinal catcher Darrell Porter was charged with a passed ball?

10. Who had the game-winning hit for the Royals, and who was he pinch-hitting for?

11. Who scored the winning run?

12. Who was the winning pitcher?

Safe at First?

12. KC's pitchers held the Cardinals to just 13 runs and the all-time low World Series team batting average, .185, for a seven-game series. What was the Royals team batting average?

13. Who was the winning pitcher for the Royals in Game 5?

14. The Royals scored 3 runs in the second inning of Game 5. Who had a 2-run triple in that inning?

15. Who was the Cardinals starter in Game 7?

The Cardinals' Tommy Herr argues his point on the controversial call at first base in Game 6.

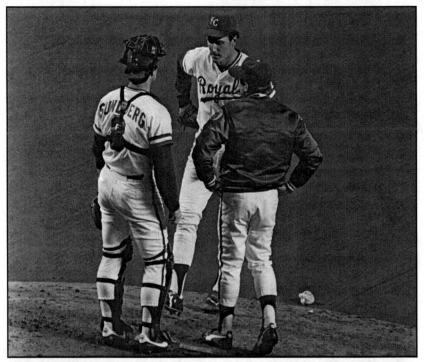

Jim Sundberg and Dick Howser confer with Charlie Leibrandt during Game 6.

Jim Sundberg eludes Cardinal catcher Darrell Porter's tag to score the winning run in Game 6. Lonnie Smith and Buddy Biancalana greet the exuberant Sundberg.

16. How many pitchers did St. Louis use in Game 7?

17. Saberhagen pitched his second complete game of the series in Game 7. How many hits did he give up?

18. How many strikeouts did Saberhagen have in Game 7?

Dan Quisenberry pitched big in Game 6 for Kansas City.

19. This player hit a 2-run home run in the second inning to put KC ahead in Game 7. Who was he?

20. Who caught the last out of the Game 7?

21. Who was the Series MVP?

22. Two Cardinals were ejected in the fifth inning of Game 7. Who were they?

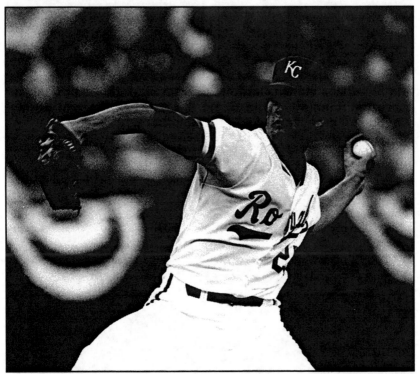

Danny Jackson pitches during Game 1 of the 1985 World Series at Royals Stadium.

Stadiums

The Royals have called two different stadiums home since the franchise entered the American League in 1969. Municipal Stadium, the club's first ballpark, never seemed a part of the club, especially since the new sports complex was under construction before the team played its first game. When the club started playing in Kauffman Stadium, Kansas City got more than just a new ballpark, it got its first winning team ever in the Major Leagues.

Municipal Stadium

1. How many years did the Royals play at Municipal Stadium?

2. What was the stadium's original name?

Municipal Stadium

Opening Day for the Monarchs, May 24, 1953. This is two years before the second deck was added.

3. What other names did the stadium go by before it was called Municipal Stadium? Who played there?

4. Where was it located?

5. What was the distance down the left field line when the Royals played there?

6. What was the distance to center field?

7. What was the distance to right field?

8. When did the Royals play their last game there?

Kauffman Stadium

1. What year did the Royals began playing in Kauffman Stadium?

2. What was its original name?

3. What year did the name change?

4. At the time of its opening, how many other American League stadiums had artificial turf?

5. Which Royals player hit the first home run in Kauffman Stadium?

6. Who threw the first no-hitter in Kauffman Stadium? When?

7. What were the original distances to the left, center and right field walls?

8. The distances to the outfield fences have been changed twice at Kauffman Stadium. When were they changed?

9. What year was real grass installed at Kauffman Stadium?

Kauffman Stadium

**1970-71
Road Uniform**

**Home Uniform for 1970s
and early 1980s**

**Road Uniform for 1970s
and early 1980s**

Uniforms

Knowing Kansas City's baseball fans might shy away from flash, odd color combinations and trend-breaking designs, Royals management opted for the conventional when it came to their new team's digs. The other 1969 expansion teams (Pilots, Padres and Expos) chose "modern" designs and colors, but the Royals' new uniforms were classic in both color and design—a far cry from the green and gold of their departed predecessor, the A's.

With just a few variances over the years—primarily polyester pullovers and elastic waist bands—the Royals have maintained a classic look on the field of play.

1985 Home Uniform

1. What sleeve patch adorned the Royals jerseys in 1969?

2. What year did the team logo sleeve patch first appear on the jerseys?

3. When did the Royals switch to polyester pullover jerseys?

4. What year did players names first adorn the back of the jerseys?

5. What year did the team return to buttoned jerseys?

6. What was on the front of the Royals first road jersey (1969)?

7. How many different cap designs have the Royals used since 1969?

1972 Road Uniform

8. The Royals have worn another team's uniform on four different occassions. Who was the team, and why?

9. In 1983 the Royals made a change to the front of their road jerseys. What was it?

10. An alternate blue jersey was introduced by the club in 1994. What specific guidelines did the team have for wearing the jersey?

11. An alternate cap was introduced and worn during the 1995 season. When did the team wear the cap?

Alternate Jersey

1990s Road Uniform

1980s Road Uniform

1969 Home Uniform

Uniform Numbers

1. What number did George Brett first wear with the Royals?

2. What number did Amos Otis wear?

3. What number did Hal McRae wear?

4. What number did Brian McRae wear?

5. What number did Paul Splittorff wear?

6. What number did Dennis Leonard wear?

7. What number did Danny Tartabull wear?

8. What number did John Mayberry wear?

9. What was Bret Saberhagen's first uniform number?

10. What number did Saberhagen change to?

11. What number did Dan Quisenberry wear?

George Brett expresses his point of view after being called out for having too much pine tar on his bat in the infamous Pine Tar Game. His home run, which put the Royals ahead of the Yankees, 5-4, was instead called an out, ending the game. The Royals protested to the American League office and the final inning was later played out at the point following Brett's home run.

Speed

The Royals have always been associated with speed. Stolen bases and aggressive base running were an integral part of the team's offense throughout the club's glory years in the 1970s and 1980s. Double steals, hit and runs, taking the extra base—Kansas City played an exciting style of baseball, and speed was a big part of the club's winning tradition.

1. How many Royals have led the league in stolen bases, who are they, and how many bases did they steal?

2. How many times have the Royals led the American League in stolen bases, and in what years?

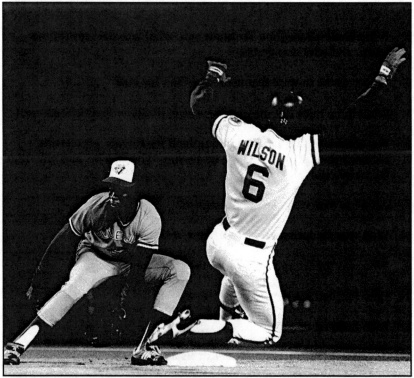

Willie Wilson slides in safely for one of his many stolen bases.

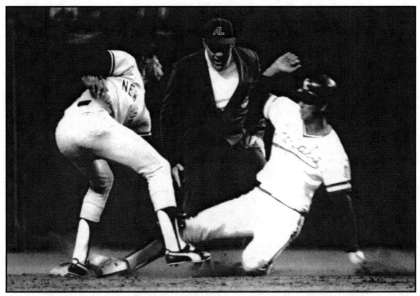

Amos Otis eludes a tag for another stolen base.

3. Who was the first Royal to steal a base?

4. Who was the first Royal to steal a base in Kauffman Stadium?

5. Who was the first Royal to steal home?

6. How many times did George Brett steal home in his career?

7. Who has stolen home the most times in Royals history, and how many times?

8. John Wathan set a stolen base record in 1982. What was it?

9. Whose record did Wathan break?

10. Who holds the Royals team record for the most career stolen bases? How many?

11. This Royals outfielder finished second in the AL in stolen bases in 1995 and 1996. Who was he, and how many bases did he steal?

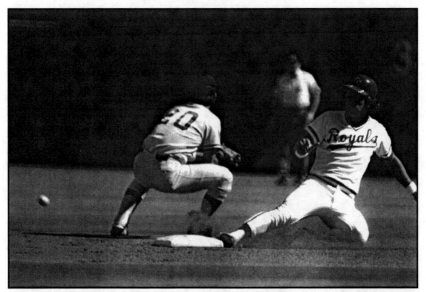

George Brett wasn't the fastest of Royals, but he was smart on the basepaths, and always ready to take an extra base or steal in a key situation. Here he slides in safely for a double against the Yankees.

12. The Royals team record for stolen bases is 218. What year did they steal this amount?

13. This speedy outfielder came to the Royals from the New York Mets and is just one of five Royals players to steal 50 or more bases in a season. Who is he?

Nicknames

What's in a name? The Royals have had a few players with memorable nicknames over the years, and a few with some you've probably never heard before. Here's a sampling of both.

1. Who was called Mullet?

2. Two different Royals were called Opie. Who were they?

3. Which pitcher was called Big Man?

4. What was Danny Jackson's nickname?

5. Freddie Patek had two nicknames. What were they?

6. What is Bo Jackson's real first name?

7. Who was called Sweetstick?

8. The Duke. Who is he?

9. What was Jim Sundberg's nickname?

10. What is Cookie Rojas' real name?

11. Who is Bye-Bye?

12. Who was called Duck, and why?

13. Who was called Spider?

14. What is Whitey Herzog's real name?

15. Who was Mr. Ribbie?

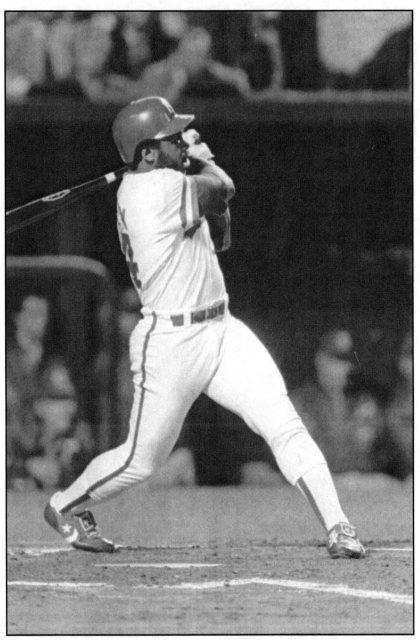

Game 7, 1985 World Series. Darryl Motley connects for one of the biggest home runs in the history of the Royals.

Home Runs

Home runs have never been a major offensive emphasis for the Royals, but there have been a few memorable ones hit by the team, and you could even say there were a few sluggers in their lineup over the years.

1. Who hit the first home run in Royals history?

2. Who hit the first grand slam in team history?

3. Who holds the Royals record for the most home runs in a season, and how many did he hit?

4. Who is the only Royals player to homer in his first official Major League at-bat?

5. Only one Royals player has ever hit three home runs in a double-header. Who is he?

6. Who hit the first pinch-hit home run in Royals history?

7. Only one Royals player has ever hit three home runs in a game at Kauffman Stadium. Who is he, and when did he do it?

8. How many Royals have hit 30 or more home runs in a season? Who are they, and how many did they hit?

9. George Brett holds the Royals record for career home runs. How many did he hit?

10. Who is second in career home runs for the Royals?

11. How many career home runs did John Mayberry hit with the Royals?

12. How many home runs did Danny Tartabull hit with KC?

Miscellaneous

1. Who was the first player selected by the Royals in the expansion draft on October 15, 1968?

2. The Royals have only defeated one opponent in every contest played during an entire season. Who was that opponent?

3. Who holds the club record for consecutive games played?

4. What is the longest game (innings) in Royals history?

5. What are the most hits recorded by the Royals in a game?

6. What is the largest shutout victory in Royals history?

7. Which two players hold the club record for hits in a game?

8. What is the largest winning margin in Royals history?

9. Who holds the club record for home runs by a lefthanded batter in a season?

10. Ewing Kauffman sold 49 percent of the Royals in 1983. Who did he sell to?

11. When did Kauffman regain full ownership of the Royals?

12. Brian McRae was a first-round draft pick in what year?

13. When did the Royals tour Japan?

14. Who comprised the Royals first radio broadcast team?

The Answers

ROYALS PLAYERS TRIVIA
George Brett
1. El Segundo High (California)
2. He singled off Stan Bahnsen
3. Ferguson Jenkins on May 8, 1974 at Texas
4. Three. 1975 with 13 (tied for 1st), 1976 with 14 and 1979 with 20
5. Twice, with 45 in both 1978 and 1990
6. 1976 and 1979
7. 1987
8. He singled off Chicago's Joel Davis at Royals Stadium on May 25, 1986
9. California's Tim Fortugno at Anaheim
10. He was picked off first base
11. One, September 28, 1980 against Minnesota. It was a grand slam.
12. Jon Matlack
13. August 29, 1982, at Comiskey Park in Chicago. It was a single off Lamar Hoyt.
14. The Indians Mark Clark on May 13, 1993, at Cleveland
15. Stan Musial, Hank Aaron, Willie Mays, Al Kaline and Carl Yastrzemski
16. Mitch Williams of the Rangers on June 1. It was also his 1,000th RBI.
17. The Indians' Mark Clark at Cleveland
18. 13 (1976-1988)
19. 11 consecutive (1976-1986)
20. Twice
21. 1980 and 1981
22. 3,154 hits
23. Tom Henke of the Texas Rangers at Arlington Stadium
24. 2,707 games
25. .305
26. Nolan Ryan & Robin Yount

Hal McRae
1. Florida A&M
2. July 11, 1968 with the Reds
3. 1977 (54) and 1982 (46)
4. Once, 1982 with 133 RBI
5. 2,091
6. Wayne Simpson came with Hal McRae to the Royals from Reds on November 30, 1972. Roger Nelson

and Richie Schienblum went to Cincinnati.
7. Hitting coach
8. .332
9. Seven (1974-76, 1982-84, 1987)
10. None
11. .000 (no hits in one official at bat, with one walk)
12. .400 (18 for 45)

Frank White
1. June 12, 1973 at Baltimore
2. Shortstop
3. June 14; a single off the Orioles' Doyle Alexander
4. June 27 at Oakland
5. April 6, 1974 (Opening Day) off Minnesota's Tom Burgmeier
6. Eight
7. 1977
8. Six (1977-1982)
9. 1978
10. Five
11. 1979
12. 2,006

Willie Wilson
1. September 4, 1976 against Texas at Royals Stadium
2. Once, with 83 in 1979
3. 21 in 1985
4. Gary Templeton
5. First major leaguer to have 700 official at bats
6. Five times (1980,1982, 1985, 1987, 1988)
7. Once, with 133 in 1980
8. One, with a batting average of .332 in 1982
9. Two, 1982 and 1983
10. Three
11. The Oakland Athletics and the Chicago Cubs

Bret Saberhagen
1. Cleveland High in Reseda, California
2. True
3. Shortstop

4. 19th
5. April 4, 1984 against the Yankees at Royals Stadium. He gave up three hits in 4.2 innings as the Royals lost, 4-3.
6. 19 years, 11 months and 24 days
7. Detroit on April 19, 1984. He beat the Tiger 5-2.
8. He was traded to the New York Mets with Bill Pecota for Greg Jeffries, Keith Miller and Kevin McReyolds.
9. Two
10. 110
11. True. He is the only Royals pitcher to win the fielding award.
12. August 26, 1991 against the White Sox at Royals Stadium

Bo Jackson

1. Steve Carlton of the White Sox
2. Mike Moore, September 14, 1986, at Royals Stadium
3. Bo led the American League in strike-outs with 172 in 1989.
4. No, he never won a Gold Glove.
5. He was the first 25-25 Royal in the club's history (25 HRs and 27SBs).
6. 1984
7. 34
8. Randy Johnson of Seattle
9. 1989
10. Rick Reuschel of the Giants
11. Homer and steal a base

Larry Gura

1. Arizona State
2. Tulsa
3. The Cubs and Yankees
4. Fran Healy
5. Eighteen. He did it twice, in 1980 and 1982
6. The Cubs
7. None. He started two games but had no decisions
8. One, in 1980
9. 2.19, best for the series
10. One, four times (1970, 1971, 1976, 1985)

Amos Otis

1. New York Mets
2. Otis came to the Royals in a trade

with Bob Johnson from the Mets for Joe Foy.
3. 1971
4. Fred Patek
5. 1973
6. Five
7. He stole five bases in one game against Milwaukee.
8. 1971
9. Three
10. Pittsburgh

Dan Quisenberry

1. July 8, 1979 against Chicago at Royals Stadium. K.C. lost, 4-2.
2. July 23, 1979 at Texas. He worked .1 inning in a 5-4 K.C. win.
3. Five (1980, 1982-85)
4. The Rolaids Fireman-of-the-Year Award
5. Had 40 or more saves two years in a row (45 in '83, 44 in '84)
6. Three – Laverne College (California), Orange Coast College (California, Junior College), and Pacific College (Fresno, California)
7. Three (1982-84)
8. No. He stared one game in the minors, for Waterloo, IA in 1975, a complete game victory, 5-3.
9. St. Louis and San Francisco
10. 573
11. Three (1980, 1983, and 1985)

Steve Busby

1. USC, where he led the Trojans to the national title in 1971.
2. September 8, 1972 against Minnesota. Steve won the game, 3-2.
3. Two, 1974 and 1975
4. Twice, 1973 and 1975
5. AL Rookie Pitcher of the Year
6. He threw a no-hitter
7. April 27, 1973 at Tiger Stadium; June 19, 1974 at Milwaukee's County Stadium
8. 70
9. None
10. 13, at Milwaukee, July 10, 1973

Dennis Leonard

1. He was their second-round pick in

the 1972 June free-agent draft
2. Oceanside High School (New York)
3. Iona College
4. September 4, 1975
5. Three
6. 106
7. He tied Nolan Ryan of California and Mike Flannagan of Baltimore with five shutouts.
8. 1977
9. Innings pitched, 201
10. 1978, 1979, 1980

Cookie Rojas
1. The Reds
2. Sandy Koufax
3. Four
4. The Phillies, 1965
5. One. A home run at Atlanta in the 1972 game.
6. Twice. 1965 (.303) with Philadelphia and 1971 (.300) with Royals
7. Kansas City acquired Cookie from the Cardinals on June 13, 1970 for Fred Rico.
8. Luis Alcarez was the Royals Opening Day second baseman in 1970.
9. The California Angels

Fred Patek
1. The Pirates
2. Jerry May and Bruce Dal Canton
3. 5'5" – He was the smallest man in major league baseball during his career.
4. Once. He had 53 in 1977 to lead the league.
5. False. He led the league once with 11 in 1971.
6. Two (1976 and 1978)
7. The Angels
8. Jim Perry
9. 385
10. .242

Mark Gubicza
1. William Penn Charter High School in Philadelphia
2. April 6, 1984 against Cleveland. He lost the game, 2-0.
3. May 12, 1984 against Boston. He pitched a four-hit shutout, winning 4-

0.
4. 132
5. Two, 1988 and 1989
6. None
7. 1988. He 20-8 for the season.
8. 14 K's against the Twins on August 27, 1988
9. Frank Viola and Dennis Eckersley

Kevin Appier
1. Fresno State University and Antelope Valley J.C.
2. He was selected in the first round of the 1987 June draft (ninth pick overall)
3. June 4, 1989 at California
4. June 13, 1989. He pitched five innings against the A's as the Royals won, 5-3.
5. June 15, 1997. He beat the Pirates 8-1 at Pittsburgh.
6. Once, 1995.
7. 2.56
8. Six, 1992-1997.
9. Once. He had 207 in 1996.
10. He struck out four batters in one inning on September 3, 1996 in Toronto. He K'd Ed Sprague, Carlos Delgado, Charlie O'Brien and Alex Gonzalez (Delgado reached first on a wild pitch).

Jeff Montgomery
1. Marshall University, where he earned a degree in Computer Science
2. From the Reds in a trade for Van Snider in 1987
3. June 4, 1988
4. One, with the Reds in 1987
5. June 8, 1988 against Oakland
6. 1993
7. Three – 1992, 1993, 1996
8. 265 through the 1997 season
9. 43

John Mayberry
1. The Astros. Kansas City sent Lance Clemmons and Jim York to Houston for Mayberry and Dave Grangaard on December 2, 1971.
2. Walks. He had 122 in 1973; 119 in 1975.

3. Twice, in 1973 and 1974
4. 143
5. One, in Game 5.
6. Twice. He did on July 1, 1975, at Texas, and again on June 1, 1977, at Toronto.
7. 1973, .420
8. Fred Lynn of the Red Sox.
9. .253
10. The New York Yankees

Paul Splittorff
1. Morningside College, where he earned a Bachelor of Science in Business Administration
2. September 23, 1970
3. June 8, 1971. He beat the Senators in Kansas City, 4-2.
4. 1973. His record was 20-11.
5. 166 wins
6. 143 losses
7. 1,057, fifth all-time for the Royals
8. 2-0. He beat the Yankees in 1976 and 1977
9. Three
10. True.

MORE TRIVIA
Ewing Kauffman
1. 1968
2. Garden City, MO
3. Navy
4. 1950
5. 1973
6. July 2, 1993

Pitchers
1. Tom Gordon
2. Dennis Leonard
3. Bret Saberhagen, 20 years and 8 days old when he started at Detroit on April 19, 1984
4. Kevin Appier. He struck out four batters in one inning on September 3, 1996 in Toronto. He K'd Ed Sprague, Carlos Delgado, Charlie O'Brien and Alex Gonzalez (Delgado reached first on a wild pitch).
5. Bret Saberhagen
6. Rich Gale won 11 games in a row in 1980

7. Paul Splittorff in 1973
8. Al Fitzmorris
9. Dennis Leonard
10. Ted Abernathy
11. Dennis Leonard with 40
12. Bob Johnson with 206 in 1970, Dennis Leonard with 244 in 1977, and Kevin Appier with 207 in 1996.
13. No
14. Bret Saberhagen, 2.16 in 1989
15. Paul Splittorff, 19 in 1974
16. Roger Nelson
17. Splittorff with 144, Gubizca with 135 and Leonard with 106
18. Kevin Appier
19. Bret Saberhagen, 1989
20. Wally Bunker
21. Saberhagen in 1985 and 1989, David Cone in 1994
22. Mark Davis
23. Gaylord Perry, 1983
24. Al Hrabosky

Catchers
1. Buck Martinez
2. Milwaukee
3. Bob Boone, 1989
4. John Wathan
5. Ellie Rodriguez
6. Darrell Porter, with 112 in 1977
7. Boston
8. Brent Mayne
9. Darrell Porter
10. Ed Hearn
11. Fran Healy

First Basemen
1. Chuck Harrison
2. Steve Balboni
3. California
4. Bob Oliver
5. John Wathan
6. Clint Hurdle
7. San Diego
8. Willie Aikens
9. Houston
10. Bob Hamelin
11. Pete LaCock
12. Kevin Seitzer
13. Toronto
14. John Mayberry and George Brett

Second Basemen
1. Jerry Adair
2. Cookie Rojas
3. Fifteen, 1976-1990
4. Terry Shumpert
5. Dave Nelson
6. Keith Lockhart
7. The Angels and White Sox
8. Keith Miller
9. U.L. Washington

Third Basemen
1. Joe Foy
2. Bob Oliver
3. Paul Schaal
4. 1974. He took over from Paul Schaal after the season started.
5. Kevin Seitzer
6. Greg Pryor
7. Gary Gaetti
8. Gary Gaetti
9. Texas
10. One, Brett in 1985

Shortstops
1. Jackie Hernandez
2. Eight. 1971, 1973-1979
3. U.L. Washington
4. Onix Concepcion and Buddy Biancalana
5. Angel Salazar
6. Danny Jackson
7. Bob Floyd
8. Greg Gagne
9. David Howard
10. Montreal and Pittsburgh
11. Frank White
12. Lance Mulliniks
13. Jackie Hernandez, Rich Severson and Tom Matchick
14. George Brett

Outfielders
1. Ed Kirkpatrick in left, Lou Piniella in center and Bob Oliver in right
2. Seattle Pilots
3. Vada Pinson
4. Jim Wohlford
5. Al Cowens
6. Tom Poquette
7. Three. Amos Otis (1971, 1973-74), Al Cowens (1977) and Willie Wilson

(1980)
8. Joe Zdeb
9. Clint Hurdle
10. Lonnie Smith
11. Scott Bankhead, Mike Kingery and Steve Shields
12. Jerry Martin
13. Al Cowens
14. Danny Tartabull
15. Vince Coleman. He had 50 steals in 1994
16. Pat Sheridan
17. August 12, 1995

Designated Hitters
1. Ed Kirkpatrick
2. Thirteen
3. Harmon Killebrew
4. Dave Nelson
5. Jorge Orta
6. Left and right field
7. Three (1976, 1980 and 1982)
8. First base
9. Orlando Cepeda
10. Lonnie Smith

Managers
1. Fourteen, counting two interim managers
2. Joe Gordon
3. Jim Frey
4. Charlie Metro
5. Three. John Wathan, Hal McRae and Bob Boone
6. Dick Howser
7. Dick Howser, 1981-1986. Whitey Herzog managed 1975-1979
8. Bob Schaefer, as an interim manager in 1991. He managed one game.
9. Whitey Herzog, .574 (410 wins, 304 losses)
10. Dick Howser, 365. But he also won 404 games
11. Whitey Herzog, Jim Frey and Dick Howser
12. They won 31 and lost 48

American League Championship Series
1976 ALCS
1. Mayberry and Brett, both in Game 5
2. Larry Gura

3. Dennis Leonard
4. Doug Bird
5. George Brett, .444
6. Hal McRae
7. Al Cowens and Jim Wohlford
8. Mark Littell
9. Five

1977 ALCS
1. Splitorff
2. McRae, Mayberry and Cowens
3. None
4. Andy Hassler
5. Leonard
6. Fred Patek
7. Dennis Leonard
8. Hal McRae
9. Reggie Jackson
10. Patek. He grounded into a game-ending double play

1978 ALCS
1. Boston, 5-4
2. Larry Gura
3. Catfish Hunter
4. Thurman Munson
5. Fred Patek
6. Dennis Leonard

1980 ALCS
1. Larry Gura
2. George Brett
3. Dennis Leonard
4. Willie Randolph
5. One, in Game 3
6. Dan Quisenberry
7. One, for Leonard in Game 2
8. Willie Wilson and U.L. Washington

1981 Divisional Playoff
1. Because of the strike, the season was divided into two halves
2. None. The A's swept them, 3-0
3. Two
4. Mike Jones
5. Larry Gura

1984 ALCS
1. Buddy Black
2. Bret Saberhagen
3. Kirk Gibson
4. Dan Quisenberry
5. Charlie Leibrandt

6. Don Slaught, .364

1985 ALCS
1. Jim Sundberg
2. Dan Quisenberry
3. One, Game 6
4. Game 1, he pitched one inning of relief
5. Two. Willie Wilson and Lonnie Smith had one each
6. Bret Saberhagen
7. Charlie Leibrandt
8. Pat Sheridan
9. Tom Henke
10. K.C. had 7, Toronto had 2
11. Three
12. Brett. He hit .348 for the series and had three HRs and five RBIs

The World Series
1980 World Series
1. Dennis Leonard
2. Amos Otis
3. Dan Quisenberry
4. Amos Otis
5. K.C. had eight, Philly had three
6. Six
7. Darrell Porter
8. Willie Aikens
9. Jose Cardenal
10. Frank White was on third, Hal McRae was on second and Amos Otis was on first. The Phillies won the game, 4-3.
11. Dennis Leonard
12. Steve Carlton, who won Games 2 and 6
13. One, in Game 3
14. Otis, .478; Hurdle, .417; Aikens, .400
15. Aikens with eight
16. Mike Schmidt had two, Bake McBride had one
17. One
18. Willie Wilson struck out, his 12th of the series—a record

1985 World Series
1. Danny Jackson
2. John Tudor
3. Leibrandt
4. Terry Pendleton
5. Frank White
6. Joaquin Andujar
7. Three. Lonnie Smith, Dane Iorg and

Jamie Quick
8. Each team hit two home runs
9. Royals had seven, the Cards had two
10. Brett hit .370, Wilson hit .367
11. Tito Landrum hit .360
12. .288
13. Danny Jackson
14. Willie Wilson
15. John Tudor
16. Seven
17. Five
18. He had two strikeouts
19. Daryl Motley
20. Motley
21. Saberhagen
22. Herzog and Andujar

Game 6 — Safe at First!
1. 1-0, St. Louis
2. Jorge Orta
3. Todd Worrell
4. Jack Clark
5. Worrell
6. Don Denkinger
7. Steve Balboni. Jack Clark let a pop foul drop. Steve then singled.
8. Sundberg bunted and Orta was forced out at third base
9. McRae
10. Dane Iorg hit for Quisenberry
11. Jim Sundberg
12. Dan Quisenberry

Stadiums
Municipal Stadium
1. Four
2. Muehlbach Stadium
3. Ruppert Stadium and Blues Stadium. The Blues and Monarchs
4. 22nd and Brooklyn in Kansas City, MO
5. 369 feet
6. 421 feet
7. 338 feet
8. October 4, 1972. Kansas City beat Texas, 4-0.

Kauffman Stadium
1. 1973
2. Royals Stadium
3. 1993
4. None
5. John Mayberry, on April 10, 1973

6. Nolan Ryan, then with the Angels, on May 15, 1973. It was the first of his career.
7. 330 feet down the lines and 405 feet to center field
8. 1980 and 1995
9. 1995

Uniforms
1. Major league baseball's 100th anniversary patch
2. 1970
3. 1973
4. 1978
5. 1983
6. Kansas City in script lettering
7. Two
8. The Kansas City Monarchs, to honor the Negro Leagues
9. Royals appeared on the front of the jerseys instead of Kansas City
10. Home Sunday games
11. On the road

Uniform Numbers
1. 25
2. 26
3. 11
4. 56
5. 34
6. 22
7. 4
8. 7
9. 31
10. 18
11. 29

The Pine Tar Game
1. July 24, 1983 at Yankee Stadium
2. Billy Martin
3. New York in the lead, 4 to 3. U.L. Washington
4. Tim McClelland, home plate
5. Rules 1.10 (b), 6.06 (d) and 2.00. Since the Pine Tar game, 1.10 (b) in essence became 1.10 (c), and a provision was added to the rule stating that a bat with too much of a grip enhancing substance was not grounds for calling a batter out.
6. Lee McPhail. He said the pine tar on Brett's bat was not a distance

enhancing substance and therefore the home run was allowed.
7. August 18, 1983 at Yankee Stadium
8. Goose Gossage
9. Mike Armstrong
10. Dan Quisenberry. He picked up his 33rd save of the year
11. George Frazier
12. Hal McRae struck out.
13. Don Mattingly flied to center, Roy Smalley flied out to deep left and Oscar Gamble grounded out to end the game.

Speed

1. Otis (1971-52), Patek (1977-53), Wilson (1979-83)
2. Six times. 1971-130, 1978-216, 1979-207, 1980-185, 1994-140, 1996-195
3. Joe Foy, on April 9, 1969 at Municipal Stadium against the Twins
4. Fred Patek, in the Stadium's first game, April 10, 1973 against the Rangers
5. Amos Otis, at California, July 31, 1972
6. Twice. August 17, 1976 vs. Cleveland and September 14, 1987 vs. California
7. John Nunnally, four times, all in 1995
8. He set the record for most stolen bases by a catcher in the major leagues with 36 thefts.
9. Ray Schalk of the Chicago White Sox
10. Willie Wilson, 612 (with the Royals)
11. Tom Goodwin, 50 in '95 and 66 in '96
12. 1978
13. Vince Coleman. He stole 50 bases in 1994

Home Runs

1. Mike Fiore hit a solo shot at Oakland on April 13, 1969
2. Bob Oliver on July 4, 1969 against Seattle
3. Steve Balboni, 36 in 1985
4. Jon Nunnally
5. Bill Pecota hit three homers in a doubleheader against the Yankees in 1989
6. Bob Taylor at Detroit, May 6, 1969
7. Danny Tartabull against Oakland on July 6, 1991
8. Eight. Steve Balboni, 36, 1985; Gary

Gaetti, 35, 1995; John Mayberry, 34, 1975; Danny Tartabull, 34, 1987 and 31, 1991; Dean Palmer, 34, 1998; Bo Jackson, 32, 1989; George Brett, 30, 1985; Chili Davis, 30, 1997.
9. 317
10. Amos Otis with 193
11. 143, from 1972 through 1977
12. 124, from 1987 through 1991

Nicknames

1. George Brett
2. Kurt Stillwell and Jerry Don Gleaton
3. Rich Gale
4. Jason
5. The Flea and Moochie
6. Vincent Edward Jackson
7. U.L. Washington
8. John Wathan
9. Sunny
10. Octavio Rojas
11. Steve Balboni
12. Marty Pattin, for his Donald Duck imitations
13. Roger Nelson
14. Dorrel Norman Elvert Herzog
15. Hal McRae

Miscellaneous

1. Roger Nelson
2. Baltimore Orioles in 1988
3. Hal McRae with 263 games
4. The Royals have played 18-inning games twice, both against the Texas Rangers. K.C. won 4-3 on June 6, 1991 and lost 4-3 on May 17, 1972
5. 24, at Detroit, June 5, 1976
6. 16-0, against Oakland on June 25, 1984
7. Bob Oliver had six hits against California on May 4, 1969, and Kevin Seitzer had six hits against Boston on August 2, 1987
8. 17 runs. The Royals beat Minnesota, 23-6, on April 6, 1974
9. John Mayberry, with 34 in 1975
10. Avron Fogelman
11. January 1991
12. 1985
13. Following the 1980 World Series
14. Buddy Blattner and Denny Mathews

PHOTO CREDITS

Alan Barzee - 7, 40(a), 57, 59, 61, 62, 63, 64, 65(a), 69, 70, 71, 120, 131, 132, 155(b)

Michael Bodenhamer - 56

George Brace - 13, 22(b), 38, 128

Corbis-Bettmann - 2, 34, 36, 140, 164

Kansas City Star - 41, 72, 73, 89

Lawrence Journal World Collection, Kansas Collection, University of Kansas Libraries - 5, 6, 11, 14, 16, 18, 19, 21, 22(a), 24, 25, 26, 28, 29, 30, 31, 33, 37, 39, 40(b), 44, 46, 52, 58, 60, 80, 83, 85, 92, 95, 96, 99, 101, 102, 107, 108, 118, 123, 124, 128, 130, 135, 136, 139, 141, 142, 143, 144, 145(b), 147, 148, 149, 158, 167, 168

National Baseball Hall of Fame - 12, 27, 32, 35, 65(b), 68,153,157, 159

Marc Okkonen - 160, 161, 162

Topeka Capital-Journal - 3, 10, 42, 45, 47, 48(b), 49, 50, 51, 52, 53, 54, 55, 76, 86, 145(a), 146, 150, 152, 154, 155(a), 156, 166, 170

Front cover photo of George Brett: Photo By USA TODAY Sports (c) Copyright USA TODAY Sports

Back cover photos of George Brett & Bret Saberhagen, 1985 World Series celebration, and Frank White: *Topeka Capital-Journal*

Acknowledgements

No matter how much I might want to do everything by myself, a project of this size can't be completed without the assistance of others.

I was lucky to have the help of some very good people who deserve recognition for efforts.

I especially want to thank Jim Donovan for his help and guidance, and also Larry Names, for thinking a book on the Royals was a worthwhile project.

I owe a big thank you to Alan Barzee, who supplied many of the photos in this book. Thanks to Pat Kelly and Darci Harrington of the photo department at the National Baseball Hall of Fame in Cooperstown. Their help was greatly appreciated. Marc Okkonnen generously allowed the use of his wonderful uniform drawings. The good people at the Society of American Baseball Research (SABR) provided a lot of needed material. Kristin Eshelman and Becky Schulte of the Kansas Collection at the University of Kansas helped me find many of the excellent photos in this book. Assistance from Bern Ketchum and Amber Webb at the Topeka Capital was invaluable, as they too helped with many of the pictures in the book. Curt Floerchinger at the Kansas City Star found some important photos, and Marci Brennan and Kevin Ritteg at Corbis-Bettmann also helped with the pictures for the book. And Annie Pratt of USA TODAY Sports Images helped with the cover image for the re-issue edition of the book.

Bobby Plappinger provided many pieces of my research material. Chris Watts pulled me out of several jams and made sure some of the important images in the book were legible. I also want to thank Jerry Vickery and Lloyd Johnson for their support. Dick Woodward, Larry Smith and Tom Shine taught me many valuable skills and lessons over the course of time—thanks guys. And a special thank you goes to Dan Consolver, whose friendship and encouragement through the years meant a great deal to me.

And finally, thanks to my wife Kathleen for her overwhelming love and support. She's the reason this book is finally seeing the light of day.

About the Author

M ark Stallard is a native Kansan who, in the days before cable TV and the internet, listened to baseball games on an old-fashioned device called a radio. *Kansas City Royals Facts & Trivia*™ was his first book, and since its original release, Mark has authored more than 10 other books, including *Tales from the Kansas Jayhawks Locker Room* and *Then Landry Said to Staubach....* He has also written for several different baseball publications and is a member of the Society of American Baseball Research (SABR).

Mark lives in the Kansas City metropolitan area with his wife, Kathleen, and their two sons.

Autographs